SOUTH EAS

Nicholas King

Capital Transport

ISBN 185414 167 8

Published by Capital Transport Publishing
38 Long Elmes, Harrow Weald, Middlesex

Printed by Bath Midway Press Ltd
Midlands Industrial Estate, Holt, Wiltshire

AUTOPOINT	4
BEE LINE	6
BEXHILL BUS COMPANY	9
BLUE LAKE	10
BLUE SALOON	11
BLUE TRIANGLE	12
BRIGHTON BLUE BUS	13
BRIGHTON & HOVE	17
CHALKWELL COACH HIRE	21
CHILTERN QUEENS	22
COASTAL COACHES	23
EASTBOURNE BUSES	24
EASTONWAYS	29
EAST SURREY	30
FARLEIGH COACHES	32
FUGGLES	33
GREY-GREEN	34
HANTS & SUSSEX	35
KENT COACH TOURS	36
MAIDSTONE & DISTRICT	38
MARCHWOOD MOTORWAYS	46
MERCURY PASSENGER SERVICES	48

Acknowledgements

The author and the publisher would like to thank Dave Stewart and the PSV Circle for assistance during the preparation of this book. The front cover photo is by Dave Stewart, the title page photo is by Tony Wilson, and the back cover photos are by Malcolm McDonald. The photos on these pages are by Phillip Stephenson.

NU-VENTURE	49
OXFORD BUS COMPANY	50
PEOPLE'S PROVINCIAL	54
POYNTER'S	58
RAMBLER	59
RDH SERVICES	61
READING BUSES	62
READING MAINLINE	66
RYE COACHES	67
SAFEGUARD	68
SMITH'S (SITTINGBOURNE)	69
SOUTHAMPTON CITYBUS	70
SOUTHERN VECTIS/SOLENT BLUE LINE	74
STAGECOACH SOUTH	82
SUSSEX BUS	98
TAPPINS	98
THAMES TRANSIT	101
THANET BUS	106
TILLINGBOURNE	107
TOWN & AROUND	110
TURNER	110
WEALDEN BEELINE	110

AUTOPOINT

B.P. Rodemark, Gardner Street, Herstmonceux, East Sussex, BN27 4LE

From small beginnings as a country minibus operator, Autopoint has expanded to a fleet of nearly 30 vehicles since deregulation in October 1986, operating a network of local bus services and contracts. Many of these are under contract to East Sussex County Council, though there were some losses in the autumn 1993 round of retendering.

Vehicle policy has shown some enterprising trends, including the operation of Leyland Cubs and Dennis Lancets. Many vehicles have been re-registered with private AP marks originally issued in West Sussex. Fleet colours are white, dark blue and light blue and the fleet is based at Bodle Street.

Most of the Autopoint fleet has received locally-based AP registrations, but a recent arrival yet to succumb to this trend is K171YVC, a Mercedes-Benz 811D with Wright bodywork new in 1992. Here it is seen at Lewes Bus Station on the East Sussex County Council service from Alfriston.
Alan Simpkins

The first of two Leyland Nationals in the fleet arrived in 1992. PVF361R, an 11.3 metre example, came from Bailey, Sutton-in-Ashfield, and is seen at Lewes Bus Station. David Harman

AUTOPOINT

	Reg	Chassis	Body	Seating	Year	History
1	JYJ173N	Ford R1014	Duple Dominant	C45F	1974	Ex Jackson, Eastbourne, 1987
2	5752AP	Bedford YMT	Duple Dominant	C53F	1976	Ex Leamland, Hassocks, 1986
3	PVF361R	Leyland National 11351A/1R		B49F	1976	Ex Bailey, Sutton-in-Ashfield, 1992
4	PKP550R	Leyland National 11351A/1R		B49F	1976	Ex Maidstone & District, 1993
5	545XFM	Leyland Leopard PSU5C/4R	Duple Dominant I	C51F	1977	Ex Maidstone & District, 1993
6	AFG249S	Ford R1114	Duple Dominant II	C53F	1978	Ex Light, London.SW19, 1989
7	5501AP	Bedford YMT	Van Hool McArdle	C53F	1978	Ex Day & Butland, Westham, 1987
8	3069AP	Ford R1014	Plaxton Supreme III	C45F	1978	Ex London Borough of Barking, 1988
9	3442AP	Leyland Leopard PSU3E/4R	Van Hool Aragon	C53F	1979	Ex Horlock, Northfleet, 1987
10	APH519T	Ford T152	Duple Dominant II	C35F	1979	Ex Airport Parking, Copthorne, 1992
11	7693AP	Mercedes-Benz L508DG	Robin Hood	C18F	1980	Ex Plumpton Coaches, Plumpton, 1990
12	1241AP	Mercedes-Benz L508D	Reeve Burgess	C21F	1982	Ex Michael, Carshalton, 1985
13	FNM739Y	Ford A0610	Mellor	B24F	1983	Ex Ash, Leatherhead, 1986
14	DBJ371Y	Ford Transit	Steedrive	B16F	1983	Ex Upper Waveney Community Bus, 1986
15	8903AP	Volvo B10M-61	Van Hool Alizée H	C49FT	1983	Ex Smith-Shearings, Wigan, 1989
16	9415AP	Mercedes-Benz L207D	Coachcraft	C12F	1983	Ex Michaels, Croydon, 1986
17	2779AP	Mercedes-Benz L608D	Robin Hood	C25F	1984	Ex Purley Car Co, Warlingham, 1984
18	7634AP	Mercedes-Benz L608D	Robin Hood	C21F	1986	
19	2317AP	Mercedes-Benz L608D	PMT	B20F	1986	Ex Southdown, 1991
20	C592SHC	Mercedes-Benz L608D	PMT	B20F	1986	Ex Southdown, 1991
21	9163AP	Bedford YMPS	Plaxton Paramount 3200 3	C33F	1987	
22	4058AP	Mercedes-Benz 709D	Advanced Vehicle Bodies	DP25F	1987	
23	D907MVU	Freight Rover 350D	Dixon Lomas	B16F	1987	Ex M Khan, Crawley, 1987
24	E863UKO	Ford Transit VE6	Dormobile	B20F	1987	Ex demonstrator, 1991
25	F361JYJ	Mercedes-Benz 609D	Reeve Burgess	DP19F	1988	
26	1509AP	Mercedes-Benz 609D	North West Coach Sales	DP24F	1989	
27	G102APC	Toyota HB31R	Caetano Optimo	C15F	1989	Ex Horseman, Reading, 1994
28	K171YVC	Mercedes-Benz 811D	Wright	B33F	1992	

Previous registrations

AFG249S	UME389S, 9925AP	5501AP	BUR428T
JYJ173N	GBM765N, 4058AP	5752AP	MPE773P
1241AP	OML730X	7634AP	C204BCR
1509AP	F255KDM	7693AP	KFG956W
2317AP	C590SHC	8903AP	ENF578Y, SPR124, GNF470Y
2779AP	A311STR	9163AP	D39WDY
3069AP	WMM100T	9415AP	A605TGO
3442AP	CTM417T	545XFM	UKR144S
4058AP	D759TTU		

THE BEE LINE

Q Drive Buses Ltd, Coldborough House, Market Street, Bracknell, Berkshire, RG12 1JA

The present company was established as the Berks Bucks Bus Co in January 1987 as a renaming of Alder Valley North. This had in turn been formed on 1st January 1986 following the division of the former Thames Valley & Aldershot Omnibus Company Ltd and was sold by the NBC to Q Drive, part of the Len Wright group, in December 1987. The present title was adopted on 9th December 1992. The trading name 'The Bee Line' is used for local bus services, together with a bee motif; minibuses operate as 'Busy Bee'. The operational area corresponds closely with that of the former Thames Valley Traction Company.

During the autumn of 1986 a number of livery experiments took place resulting in the adoption of golden yellow with dark grey skirt for local buses, and variants have been developed for minibus operations.

Operations in the High Wycombe area were transferred to Oxford Bus Company in November 1990. The Londonlink service went to Reading Transport in October 1991 and operations at Newbury and Reading followed in July 1992. Work in the Slough area was taken over from Luton & District in January 1993.

The present head office was occupied in January 1994. The fleet is operated from depots at Bracknell, Maidenhead and Slough.

In 1988 Bee Line purchased five Leyland Olympians with Northern Counties bodywork, chiefly for use on the Reading to Slough and Windsor corridor. No.602, at Heathrow Airport in February 1994, demonstrates the eastward extent of this important trunk route. Colin Lloyd

There is still a sizeable contingent of Leyland Nationals in the fleet, some vehicles twenty years old. One of the newer examples is No.365, photographed in Slough on 10th August 1992. Malcolm MacDonald

THE BEE LINE

| 112 | E982DNK | MCW Metrorider MF150/81 | MCW | B23F | 1988 | Ex Luton & District, 1993 |
| 113 | E983DNK | MCW Metrorider MF150/81 | MCW | B23F | 1988 | Ex Luton & District, 1993 |

161-182
Mercedes-Benz 609D — Robin Hood — B20F — 1987 — 175 ex London Buslines, 1990

161	E457CGM	167	E463CGM	171	E467CGM	176	E472CGM	180	E476CGM
162	E458CGM	168	E464CGM	173	E469CGM	177	E473CGM	181	E477CGM
165	E461CGM	169	E465CGM	174	E470CGM	178	E474CGM	182	E478CGM
166	E462CGM	170	E466CGM	175	E471CGM	179	E475CGM		

| 191 | K379DBL | Mercedes-Benz 709D | Plaxton Beaver | B23F | 1992 |

201-208
Dennis Dart 9.8SDL3017 — Plaxton Pointer — B40F — 1993-94

| 201 | K279XJB | 203 | K282XJB | 205 | L205GMO | 207 | L207GMO |
| 202 | K281XJB | 204 | K283XJB | 206 | L206GMO | 208 | L208GMO |

302-317
Leyland National 1151/1R/0402 — B49F — 1973-74 Ex Thames Valley & Aldershot, 1986

| 302 | NRD134M | 311 | NRD152M | 313 | NRD154M | 317 | NRD160M |
| 304 | NRD136M | 312 | NRD153M | 316 | NRD159M | | |

326-352
Leyland National 11351/1R — B49F — 1974-75 Ex Thames Valley & Aldershot, 1986

| 326 | TBL170M | 331 | UMO178N | 342 | HPK501N | 348 | KPA362P | 350 | KPA376P |
| 329 | TBL174M | 336 | GPC736N | 347 | KPA360P | 349 | KPA370P | 352 | KPA381P |

355-365 Leyland National 11351A/1R | | | | | | B49F | 1976-78 Ex Thames Valley & Aldershot, 1986
359 ex Alder Valley, 1990

355	NPJ473R	359	NPJ484R	363	TPE164S	365	TPE167S
358	PPM896R	362	TPE162S	364	TPE165S		

372	LPF599P	Leyland National 11351/1R/SC				DP45FL	1976	Ex Thames Valley & Aldershot, 1986
374	LPF601P	Leyland National 11351/1R/SC				DP45FL	1976	Ex Thames Valley & Aldershot, 1986
381	LPF602P	Leyland National 11351/1R/SC				B45F	1976	Ex Thames Valley & Aldershot, 1986

400-444 Leyland National 10351B/1R | | | | | | B41F | 1978 | Ex Luton & District, 1993

400	YPL400T	406	YPL406T	416	YPL416T	429	YPL429T	444	YPL444T
401	YPL401T	407	YPL407T	422	YPL422T	432	YPL432T		
402	YPL402T	414	YPL414T	428	YPL428T	442	YPL442T		

447-465 Leyland National 10351A/1R | | | | | | B41F | 1977-78 Ex Luton & District, 1993

447	UPB297S	453	UPB303S	460	UPB320S	463	YPF763T
452	UPB302S	457	UPB307S	462	UPB352S	465	YPF765T

488	YPL388T	Leyland National 10351B/1R				B41F	1978	Ex Luton & District, 1993
503	AAA503C	Dennis Loline III	Weymann			H39/29F	1964	Ex Alder Valley, 1992

521-560 Bristol VRT/SL3/6LXB | Eastern Coach Works | | | H43/31F | 1978-80 Ex Thames Valley & Aldershot, 1992

521	VPF286S	526	WJM831T	533	CJH144V	540	GGM90W	560	GGM107W
525	WJM830T	532	CJH143V	539	GGM89W	559	GGM84W		

562	CJH122V	Bristol VRT/SL3/6LXB	Eastern Coach Works	CH39/27F	1980	Ex Thames Valley & Aldershot, 1986

601-605 Leyland Olympian ONCL10/1RZ Northern Counties | | | H45/29F | 1988

601	F172LBL	602	F173LBL	603	F174LBL	604	F175LBL	605	F176LBL

719	GGM75W	Leyland Leopard PSU3F/4R	Plaxton Supreme IV Exp	C49F	1981	Ex Thames Valley & Aldershot, 1986
724	SMY631X	Leyland Tiger TRCTL11/3R	Plaxton Supreme V	C50F	1982	Ex Luton & District, 1993
726	SMY632X	Leyland Tiger TRCTL11/3R	Plaxton Supreme V	C50F	1982	Ex Luton & District, 1993
727	SMY637X	Leyland Tiger TRCTL11/3R	Plaxton Supreme V	C50F	1982	Ex Luton & District, 1993
728	A109EPA	Leyland Tiger TRCTL11/3R	Plaxton Paramount3200Exp	C53F	1983	Ex Luton & District, 1993

740-746 Scania K113CRB | Berkhof Excellence 2000 | C53F | 1991

740	J740TDP	742	J742TDP	744	J744TDP	746	J746TDP
741	J741TDP	743	J743TDP	745	J745TDP		

752	YPJ203Y	Leyland Tiger TRCTL11/3R	Plaxton Paramount 3500	C50F	1983	Ex Thames Valley & Aldershot, 1986
754	YPJ206Y	Leyland Tiger TRCTL11/3R	Plaxton Paramount 3500	C50F	1983	Ex Alder Valley, 1992
761	A211DPB	Leyland Tiger TRCTL11/3RH	Plaxton Paramount 3200	C51F	1983	Ex Thames Valley & Aldershot, 1986
762	A212DPB	Leyland Tiger TRCTL11/3RH	Plaxton Paramount 3200	C51F	1983	Ex Thames Valley & Aldershot, 1986
765	A215DPB	Leyland Tiger TRCTL11/3RH	Plaxton Paramount 3200	C51F	1983	Ex Thames Valley & Aldershot, 1986
766	B294KPF	Leyland Tiger TRCTL11/3R	Plaxton Paramount 3200 2	C51F	1985	Ex Luton & District, 1993
767	B295KPF	Leyland Tiger TRCTL11/3R	Plaxton Paramount 3200 2	C51F	1985	Ex Luton & District, 1993
768	E322OMG	Leyland Tiger TRCTL11/3R	Plaxton Paramount 3200 3	C53F	1988	Ex Luton & District, 1993
769	C258SPC	Leyland Tiger TRCTL11/3R	Duple 320	C53F	1986	Ex Luton & District, 1993

782-789 Volvo B10M-60 | Jonckheere Jubilee P50 | C53F | 1989 | Ex Alder Valley, 1992

782	F772OJH	783	F773OJH	786	F756OJH	788	F758OJH	789	F759OJH

790	F760OJH	Volvo B10M-60	Jonckheere Jubilee P50	C53F	1989	
801	K801CAN	Leyland Lynx LX2R11C15Z4S	Leyland	B47F	1992	Ex Alder Valley, 1992
802	K802CAN	Leyland Lynx LX2R11C15Z4S	Leyland	B47F	1992	Ex Alder Valley, 1992

Special liveries
Railair Link : 740-6
Overall advertisement : 407/16/62
Traditional Aldershot & District livery : 503

8

BEXHILL BUS COMPANY

M.J. Harmer, Wrestwood Road, Bexhill-on-Sea, East Sussex, TN40 2LP

The long-established coaching firm of Renown European was responsible for baling out a consortium of former Maidstone & District employees who had set up a network of local services at Bexhill in December 1980. Operations were taken over in November 1981 and the combined fleet was operated from the present site at Wrestwood Road, Bexhill. In due course the Leyland Nationals involved were replaced by Leyland Panthers acquired from Eastbourne. These were succeeded by Bristol REs from Hastings & District.

Since October 1986 the bus side of the business has also undertaken contract operations for East Sussex County Council in the rural area, and from September 1987 co-ordinated operation was introduced with Hastings & District (now part of South Coast Buses) on the main route between Hastings, Bexhill and Sidley.

The bus fleet is generally painted cream and blue; the coach fleet remains identifiably separate in a white, grey, black and gold scheme.

The current bus fleet of Bexhill Bus Company is centred on Bristol REs with ECW bodies acquired from Hastings & District in 1990. HHW916L, photographed at Town Hall Square, Bexhill on the service from Sidley to Hastings operated in conjunction with South Coast Buses, carries a livery based on that used by Hastings & District up to their submersion in the Stagecoach fold.
John Grubb

BEXHILL BUS COMPANY

24	A904MHC	Bedford YNT	Plaxton Paramount 3200	C53F	1984	
25	A132MBA	Leyland Tiger TRCTL11/3RZ	Plaxton Paramount 3500	C49FT	1984	Ex Boro'line Maidstone, 1989
410	MVT210K	Bristol RELH6L	Eastern Coach Works	B49F	1972	Ex Hastings & District, 1990
412	AHT212J	Bristol RELL6L	Eastern Coach Works	B50F	1971	Ex Hastings & District, 1990
416	HHW916L	Bristol RELL6L	Eastern Coach Works	B50F	1972	Ex Hastings & District, 1990
417	NLJ517M	Bristol LH6L	Eastern Coach Works	B43F	1973	Ex Manxtree, Bexhill, 1984
423	PVT223L	Bristol RELL6L	Eastern Coach Works	B53F	1973	Ex Hastings & District, 1990
428	PVT228L	Bristol RELL6L	Eastern Coach Works	B53F	1973	Ex Hastings & District, 1990
	NDY269R	Bedford YMT	Duple Dominant I	C53F	1976	
	SKR556R	Leyland National 11351A/1R		B49F	1977	Ex Maidstone & District, 1994
	UMJ452W	Bedford YMQS	Plaxton Supreme IV	C37F	1981	
	GPX585X	Mercedes-Benz L508D	Robin Hood	DP19F	1982	Ex Transcity, Sidcup, 1990
	LDZ9430	DAF MB200DKTL600	Van Hool Alizée	C48FT	1982	Ex Logan, Dunley, 1994
	VKN832X	Leyland Leopard PSU3F/4R	Willowbrook 003 Mk2	DP47F	1982	Ex Maidstone & District, 1994
	VKN834X	Leyland Leopard PSU3F/4R	Willowbrook 003 Mk2	DP47F	1982	Ex Maidstone & District, 1994
	HEW312Y	Mercedes-Benz L508D	Reeve Burgess	C19F	1983	
	A844UGB	Volvo B10M-61	Van Hool Alizée H	C49FT	1984	
	A408GPY	Kässbohrer Setra S228DT	Kässbohrer Imperial	CH54/20CT	1984	Ex Zebra, Trimdon Grange, 1988
	B88AMH	Leyland Tiger TRCTL11/3R	Van Hool Alizée	C53F	1984	Ex Sault & Roff, London SE15, 1989
	C602PUF	Mercedes-Benz L608D	Reeve Burgess	B16FL	1985	Ex Community Transport, Hove, 1991
	H538CTR	Leyland Cub ST2R44C97A4	Wadham Stringer Vanguard II	B34FL	1990	

Previous registrations
LDZ9430   FRP831X, TIA5734, ADU235X

BLUE LAKE

Tramcourt Ltd, Quarry Lane, Chichester, West Sussex, PO19 2PR

Under the ownership of J. A. Redford, Blue Lake has for some years operated a town service in Chichester. Numbered 59, the route takes in East Broyle Estate and Summersdale. Operations were taken over by Tramcourt Ltd in September 1993, using the same operating centre at Quarry Lane, Chichester.

New to Southdown, Blue Lake's TCD490J worked for Sussex Bus before reaching its present owner in 1993. The combination of Bristol RESL6L chassis with Marshall bodywork is an unusual blend. This view was taken in Chichester on 20th April 1994. Gerald Mead

BLUE LAKE COACHES

VLW545G	AEC Merlin 4P2R	Metro-Cammell-Weymann	B41D	1969	Ex White Heather, Bognor Regis, 1989
BPH106H	AEC Swift 4MP2R	Park Royal	B38D	1970	Ex Dinner, Launceston, 1989
TCD490J	Bristol RESL6L	Marshall Camagna	B45F	1970	Ex Sussex Bus, Pagham, 1993
TGW893R	Bedford YMT	Plaxton Supreme	C53F	1977	Ex Tentrek, Sidcup, 1983
JFP176V	Ford R1114	Duple Dominant II	C53F	1980	Ex West, Woodford Green, 1986
LNM511V	Bedford YMT	Duple Dominant II	C53F	1980	Ex Carlone, Godalming, 1994
DLB789Y	Bova EL26/581	Bova Europa	C53F	1983	Ex Athelstan, Malmesbury, 1989
E459ANC	Mercedes-Benz 609D	Made-to-Measure	DP24F	1988	

BLUE SALOON

ABC Taxis (J. Lambley) Ltd, GB House, Westfield Road, Guildford, Surrey, GU1 1RR

This company's stage operations started on 1st March 1973 with a local Guildford service, gained after fierce competition for the licence with London Country and Tillingbourne Bus. The long-established business of Warner's Coaches, Milford was acquired on 1st August 1983.

Blue Saloon has expanded its interests since deregulation, including tendered operation in the Farnham area. An extensive programme of holidays, tours and excursions is also maintained under the trading name of GB Tours, reflecting former co-operation with Gastonia Coaches of Cranleigh. The fleet is painted in blue and white livery.

The Blue Saloon fleet includes seven ageing Bristol LHs with various styles and makes of bodywork. TPJ61S, new to London Country, arrived from a local school in 1990, and is seen in Guildford.
Malcolm McDonald

BLUE SALOON

	Reg	Chassis	Body	Seating	Year	Notes
1	KPB881P	Bristol LH6L	Eastern Coach Works	B43F	1975	
2	KPM429P	Bristol LH6L	Plaxton Supreme IIIExp	C45F	1975	
3	KJD427P	Bristol LH6L	Eastern Coach Works	B39F	1976	Ex Davies, Carmarthen, 1985
4	TMJ637R	Bristol LHL6L	Plaxton Supreme III	C53F	1976	Ex Crawt, Guildford, 1989
5	TPJ61S	Bristol LHS6L	Eastern Coach Works	B35F	1977	Ex Hurstwood House School, 1990
6	VDV107S	Bristol LH6L	Eastern Coach Works	B43F	1978	Ex National Coal Board, Yorkshire, 1985
7	VRY724S	Bedford YMT	Plaxton Supreme III	C53F	1978	Ex Warner, Milford, 1983
8	YPH406T	Bedford YMT	Plaxton Supreme IV	C53F	1978	
9	YPH407T	Bedford YMT	Plaxton Supreme IV	C53F	1978	
10	YPB820T	Bedford YMT	Plaxton Supreme IV	C53F	1978	
11	CPD131T	Bristol LH6L	Eastern Coach Works	B43F	1979	
12	HPB814V	Bedford YMT	Plaxton Supreme IV	C53F	1980	
13	KPC405W	Bedford YMT	Duple Dominant IV	C53F	1980	Ex Warner, Milford, 1983
14	HBH426Y	Leyland Tiger TRCTL11/3R	Plaxton Paramount 3200	C53F	1983	
15	776WME	Leyland Royal Tiger B54	Roe Doyen	C46FT	1984	
16	1311VY	Leyland Royal Tiger B50	Van Hool Alizée	C53F	1985	
17	OYD693	Hestair Duple 425	Duple 425	C57F	1989	

Previous registrations
OYD693   G602LKU

Special liveries
Hoppa-Shoppa : KPB881P, KJD427P, TPJ61S, VDV107S, CPD131T

BLUE TRIANGLE

R.L. Wright, Unit 3C, Denver Industrial Estate, Ferry Lane, Rainham, Essex, RM13 9BU

Blue Triangle bought out Haven Coaches of Newhaven on 16th January 1994. Haven Coaches had developed from an operation started on 29th July 1991 by D.P. Mulpeter and G.P. Marshall between Newhaven and Brighton. In January 1992 Marshall had been replaced in the partnership by R.H. Cutbush, who had applied for local registrations in his own right in the autumn of 1991 as Newhaven & District Motor Services.

The fleet has been characterised by ex-London vehicles, including Routemaster operations. Since the takeover by Blue Triangle some exchange of vehicles has taken place with the parent operation at Rainham and this is likely to continue. The Newhaven fleet is based at Newhaven Industrial Estate.

Much of the Haven Coaches fleet had been built up around former London Fleetlines in 1992 and 1993. GHV69N, an increasingly-rare example of Park Royal bodywork in the area, passes through Brighton on its way to Seaford looking somewhat battle-scarred.
Alan Simpkins

BLUE TRIANGLE BUSES Newhaven-based fleet

LDS282A	AEC Routemaster 5RM	Park Royal	H36/28R	1960	Ex Wright, Rainham, 1994
WLT933	AEC Routemaster 5RM	Park Royal	H36/28R	1961	Ex Western Scottish, 1991
MLH426L	Daimler Fleetline CRL6	MCW	H44/24D	1973	Ex London Buses, 1993
YNA349M	Daimler Fleetline CRG6LXB	Northern Counties	H43/32F	1974	Ex Burrows, Ogmore Vale, 1993
GHV962N	Daimler Fleetline CRL6	Park Royal	H44/27D	1974	Ex Q Drive, 1993
GHV40N	Daimler Fleetline CRL6	Park Royal	H44/27D	1975	Ex Q Drive, 1993
GHV69N	Daimler Fleetline CRL6	Park Royal	H45/28D	1975	Ex Wright, Rainham, 1993
GHV83N	Daimler Fleetline CRL6	Park Royal	H44/27D	1975	Ex Q Drive, 1993
KJD433P	Bristol LH6L	Eastern Coach Works	B39F	1976	Ex London Buses, 1993
KUC180P	Daimler Fleetline CRL6	Park Royal	H44/32F	1975	Ex Kirk, Pulborough, 1993
OKW503R	Leyland Fleetline FE30AGR	MCW	H45/25D	1977	Ex Cowie, London N16, 1993
OJD66R	Bristol LH6L	Eastern Coach Works	B39F	1977	Ex London Buses, 1993
OJD84R	Bristol LH6L	Eastern Coach Works	B39F	1977	Ex London Buses, 1993
OJD254R	Leyland Fleetline FE30ALRSp	MCW	H44/24D	1977	Ex London Buses, 1992
OJD264R	Leyland Fleetline FE30ALRSp	MCW	H44/24D	1977	Ex London Buses, 1992
OJD386R	Leyland Fleetline FE30ALRSp	Park Royal	H44/24D	1977	Ex London Buses, 1992
OJD438R	Leyland Fleetline FE30ALRSp	Park Royal	H44/24D	1977	Ex London Buses, 1993
THX174S	Leyland National 10351A/2R		B36D	1977	Ex Wright, Rainham, 1994
THX314S	Leyland Fleetline FE30ALRSp	MCW	H44/24D	1978	Ex Kinch, Barrow-upon-Soar, 1993
THX337S	Leyland Fleetline FE30ALRSp	MCW	H44/24D	1978	Ex London Buses, 1992
THX590S	Leyland Fleetline FE30ALRSp	Park Royal	H44/27D	1978	Ex Wright, Rainham, 1994
THX639S	Leyland Fleetline FE30ALRSp	Park Royal	H44/27D	1978	Ex Kinch, Barrow-upon-Soar, 1993

Previous registration
LDS282A   VLT245

BRIGHTON BLUE BUS

Brighton Transport Ltd, Coombe Terrace, Lewes Road, Brighton, BN2 4AQ

Brighton Blue Bus derives from the former Brighton Corporation operation which opened on 25th November 1901 with a network of 25 trams. Motor-buses were introduced on 1st April 1939, followed in May by trolleybuses. Trams were withdrawn on 31st August 1939 and trolleybuses last ran on 31st December 1960. For many years pooling arrangements were conducted with Brighton, Hove & District and also latterly with Southdown.

Deregulation in October 1986 was anticipated by the adoption in March 1986 of subsidiaries covering Brighton Buses, Brighton Coaches and, for non-operational activities, Brighton Transport. The 11-vehicle fleet of Chapman, Lewes was purchased in May 1988 and the fleetname of Lewes Coaches retained for operations. On 30th June 1989 the Campings Luxury Coaches business was purchased and continues as a separate division. Vehicles for the Lewes operation have been integrated gradually into the main fleet. The present company title was introduced in December 1993 and the fleetname Brighton Blue Bus in May 1994.

The fleet operates in a livery of light blue and white with dark blue skirt and lining and black window-surrounds. Vehicles are kept at the garage in Lewes Road, Brighton with outstations at Meadow Road, Worthing, and at Cliffe Industrial Estate, Lewes.

The Leyland Atlanteans which were long associated with the Brighton fleet are now reduced to the last batch of fifteen, purchased in 1978 with East Lancs bodywork. No.6 stands at Brighton Open Market in June 1994 displaying the new style of fleetname recently introduced. Andrew Gainsbury

The appearance of single-deckers in the Brighton fleet commenced with Leyland Nationals in 1983 and was followed by deliveries of Leyland Lynxes later in the decade. No.46, photographed in June 1994, shows the application of current livery to the Shuttle 50 service. Andrew Gainsbury

Seven Dennis Darts with Plaxton bodywork delivered in 1992 had to occupy non-sequential fleet numbers because of the lack of an adequate consecutive run of clear numbers. No.87 was photographed with the former fleetname style now being superseded. *Malcolm King*

Brighton's seven Leyland Nationals were all Mk2 models, delivered in 1983. No.30, photographed on 8th May 1993 at East Grinstead provides evidence of the operator's expansion into rural areas. *Malcolm McDonald*

The minibus era in Brighton is represented by a batch of fifteen Renault Dodge machines with Alexander bodywork delivered in 1987 and 1988. No.51 carries new fleetnames in this view at Brighton Open Market in June 1994. Andrew Gainsbury

Dennis Dominator No.20, bodied by East Lancs, is one of two fitted with dual-purpose seating for use on high-capacity private hire work when required, and so is painted with Brighton Coaches logos. It takes a turn on bus work when not otherwise required, as shown here. Malcolm King

BRIGHTON BLUE BUS

1-15
Leyland Atlantean AN68A/1R · East Lancs · H43/31F · 1978

1	TYJ1S	4	TYJ4S	7	TYJ7S	10	TYJ10S	13	TYJ13S
2	TYJ2S	5	TYJ5S	8	TYJ8S	11	TYJ11S	14	TYJ14S
3	TYJ3S	6	TYJ6S	9	TYJ9S	12	TYJ12S	15	TYJ15S

16	OAP16W	Dennis Dominator DDA134	East Lancs	H43/31F	1981	
17	OAP17W	Dennis Dominator DDA134	East Lancs	H43/31F	1981	
18	C718NCD	Dennis Dominator DDA1005	East Lancs	H43/32F	1985	
19	C719NCD	Dennis Dominator DDA1005	East Lancs	H43/32F	1985	
20	C720NCD	Dennis Dominator DDA1004	East Lancs	DPH43/28F	1985	
21	C721NCD	Dennis Dominator DDA1004	East Lancs	DPH43/28F	1985	
24	SPN669X	Leyland Leopard PSU3E/4R	Duple Dominant IV	C53F	1982	Ex Southend, 1988

25-31
Leyland National 2 NL116HLXB/1R · B49F* · 1983 · * 28-30 are B47F

25	XFG25Y	27	XFG27Y	29	XFG29Y	31	XFG31Y
26	XFG26Y	28	XFG28Y	30	XFG30Y		

33	BCD814L	Leyland National 1151/1R/0102		B49F	1973	Ex Eastbourne, 1989
36	H536CTR	Leyland Swift LBM	Wadham Stringer Vanguard II	B26FL	1990	On extended loan from East Sussex CC
37	H537CTR	Leyland Swift LBM	Wadham Stringer Vanguard II	B26FL	1990	On extended loan from East Sussex CC
38	F538LUF	Leyland Lynx LX112L10ZR1R	Leyland	B47F	1989	
44	F544LUF	Leyland Lynx LX112L10ZR1R	Leyland	B47F	1989	
45	F545LUF	Leyland Lynx LX112L10ZR1R	Leyland	B47F	1989	
46	F546LUF	Leyland Lynx LX112L10ZR1R	Leyland	B47F	1989	
47	E447FWV	Leyland Lynx LX1126LXCTZR1S	Leyland	B47F	1988	
48	E448FWV	Leyland Lynx LX1126LXCTZR1S	Leyland	B47F	1988	
49	E449FWV	Leyland Lynx LX1126LXCTZR1S	Leyland	B47F	1988	

50-64
Renault-Dodge S56 · Alexander AM · B23F* · 1987-88 * 59/60 are DP25F

50	E450OAP	53	E453WJK	56	D456YPN	59	E459WJK	62	E462CWV
51	E451OAP	54	D454YPN	57	D457YPN	60	E460WJK	63	E463CWV
52	E452OAP	55	D455YPN	58	E458WJK	61	E461CWV	64	E464CWV

67	OYJ67R	Leyland Atlantean AN68/1R	East Lancs	H45/32F	1977	
74	8683LJ	Dennis Javelin 11SDL1905	Duple 320	C53F	1988	
75	OJI8786	Dennis Javelin 11SDL1905	Duple 320	C53F	1988	
80	J980JNJ	Dennis Dart 9.8SDL3017	Plaxton Pointer	B40F	1992	
81	PIB5144	Leyland Leopard PSU3E/4RT	Willowbrook Warrior(1991)	B48F	1980	Ex Southend, 1988
83	J983JNJ	Dennis Dart 9.8SDL3017	Plaxton Pointer	B40F	1992	
84	J984JNJ	Dennis Dart 9.8SDL3017	Plaxton Pointer	B40F	1992	
85	PIB5145	Leyland Leopard PSU3E/4RT	Willowbrook Warrior(1991)	B48F	1980	Ex Southend, 1988
86	J986JNJ	Dennis Dart 9.8SDL3017	Plaxton Pointer	B40F	1992	
87	J987JNJ	Dennis Dart 9.8SDL3017	Plaxton Pointer	B40F	1992	
88	J988JNJ	Dennis Dart 9.8SDL3017	Plaxton Pointer	B40F	1992	
89	J989JNJ	Dennis Dart 9.8SDL3017	Plaxton Pointer	B40F	1992	

92-96
Leyland Lynx LX112L10ZR1R · Leyland · B47F · 1990

92	G992VWV	93	G993VWV	94	G994VWV	95	G995VWV	96	G996VWV

97	H909SKW	Renault S75	Whittaker-Europa	B29F	1990	
107	TSV717	Bedford YNT	Plaxton Paramount 3200	C53F	1984	Ex Camping, Brighton, 1989
111	OJI8785	Bedford YNT	Plaxton Paramount 3200	C53F	1984	Ex Pathfinder, Chadwell Heath, 1990

Previous registrations
OJI8785	A840PPP
OJI8786	E475FWV
PIB5144	UTD203T
PIB5145	UTD204T
TSV717	B272HCD
8683LJ	E474FWV

Special liveries
Campings : 111

Overall advertisements : 5, 17-9, 21, 27, 38, 58/9, 86, 94

Lewes Coaches 24/8-30/3, 59, 74/5, 85, 107

County Rider: 36/7

BRIGHTON & HOVE

Brighton & Hove Bus & Coach Co Ltd, Conway Street, Hove, East Sussex, BN3 3LT

The present fleetname was adopted from 21st April 1986 following the transfer of the Brighton and Hove activities of Southdown into a separate division on 1st March 1985. The former Brighton, Hove & District Ltd company had been reactivated from 1st January 1986 for the purpose. The firm was sold by the National Bus Company to a management-led team in May 1987, and absorbed within the Go-Ahead Group on 17th November 1993.

From the autumn of 1985 the fleet was gradually repainted into a distinctive new livery of cream with black skirt and dark red bands on the lower panels flying to the roof at the rear axle. The fleet was also renumbered from the former Southdown system into a three-digit scheme. An elderly Bristol KSW6G was retrieved from private ownership in 1986 and carries traditional livery.

The fleet is housed in garages at Hove and Whitehawk and at outstations in Newhaven, Shoreham and Steyning.

When the time came to replace the first generation of minibuses, a number of relatively new Mercedes-Benz with Wadham Stringer bodies were available from Bournemouth, where their introduction had been less than successful. No.348 is an example. Calvin Churchill

Replacement of older double-deckers was assisted in 1986 by the purchase of three standard Bristol VRTs with Eastern Coach Works bodies from Milton Keynes City Bus. No.277 is seen at Whitehawk in April 1994. Gerald Mead

Following management buy-out, Brighton & Hove embarked on a policy of purchasing Scania double-deckers with East Lancs bodies, taking thirty examples in a three-year span from 1988 to 1990 as well as four second-hand examples from Leicester. No.714 from the 1989 batch was photographed in Eastbourne in May 1994. Gerald Mead

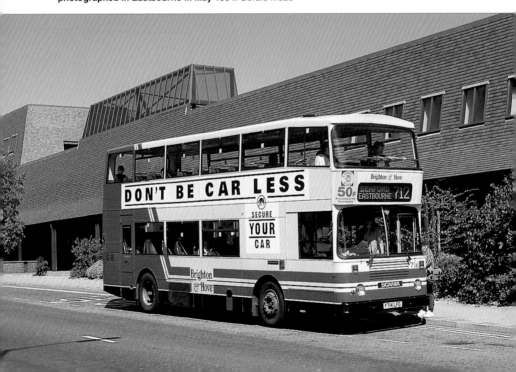

When Brighton & Hove was created from the Brighton operations of Southdown in 1986, ten of the newer Leyland National 2s formed part of the transferred fleet. No.154 was one of eight new in 1985, amongst the last of the type built, and is seen passing Sussex University at Falmer on 26th March 1994. Andrew Gainsbury

BRIGHTON & HOVE

110	C110UBC	Scania N112DR	East Lancs	H46/33F	1986	Ex Leicester, 1989
111	C111UBC	Scania N112DR	East Lancs	H46/33F	1986	Ex Leicester, 1989
112	C112UBC	Scania N112DR	East Lancs	H46/33F	1986	Ex Leicester, 1989
113	C113UBC	Scania N112DR	East Lancs	H46/33F	1986	Ex Leicester, 1989
127	JWV127W	Leyland National 2 NL116L11/1R		B52F	1980	Ex Southdown, 1986
128	JWV128W	Leyland National 2 NL116L11/1R		B52F	1980	Ex Southdown, 1986

150-157

	Leyland National 2 NL116HLXCT/1R		B49F	1985	Ex Southdown, 1986

150	C450OAP	152	C452OAP	154	C454OAP	156	C456OAP
151	C451OAP	153	C453OAP	155	C455OAP	157	C457OAP

205	C205PCD	Mercedes-Benz L608D	Alexander AM	B20F	1985	Ex Southdown, 1986
206	C206PCD	Mercedes-Benz L608D	Alexander AM	B20F	1985	Ex Southdown, 1986
210	C210PCD	Mercedes-Benz L608D	Alexander AM	B20F	1985	Ex Southdown, 1986

250-265

	Bristol VRT/SL3/6LXB		Eastern Coach Works	H43/31F	1980-81	Ex Southdown, 1986

250	JWV250W	259	JWV259W	261	JWV261W	263	JWV263W	265	JWV265W
257	JWV257W	260	JWV260W	262	JWV262W	264	JWV264W		

270	JWV270W	Bristol VRT/SL3/680	Eastern Coach Works	H43/31F	1981	Ex Southdown, 1986
272	JWV272W	Bristol VRT/SL3/680	Eastern Coach Works	H43/31F	1981	Modified to Gardner 6LXB Ex Southdown, 1986
273	JWV273W	Bristol VRT/SL3/680	Eastern Coach Works	H43/31F	1981	Modified to Gardner 6LXB Ex Southdown, 1986
277	VVV964W	Bristol VRT/SL3/6LXB	Eastern Coach Works	H43/31F	1981	Modified to Gardner 6LXB Ex Milton Keynes City Bus, 1986
278	VVV958W	Bristol VRT/SL3/6LXB	Eastern Coach Works	H43/31F	1981	Ex Milton Keynes City Bus, 1986
279	VVV959W	Bristol VRT/SL3/6LXB	Eastern Coach Works	H43/31F	1981	Ex Milton Keynes City Bus, 1986

340-359 Mercedes-Benz 811D Wadham Stringer Wessex B31F* 1989 Ex Bournemouth, 1990
* 359 is DP31F

340	F40XPR	344	F44XPR	348	F48XPR	352	G52BEL	356	G56BEL
341	F41XPR	345	F45XPR	349	F49XPR	353	G53BEL	357	G57BEL
342	F42XPR	346	F46XPR	350	G50BEL	354	G54BEL	359	G59BEL
343	F43XPR	347	F47XPR	351	G51BEL	355	G55BEL		

407	C377PCD	Leyland Tiger TRCTL11/3RH	Plaxton Paramount 3500 2	C49FT	1986
408	C378PCD	Leyland Tiger TRCTL11/3RH	Plaxton Paramount 3500 2	C49FT	1986
409	C379PCD	Leyland Tiger TRCTL11/3RH	Plaxton Paramount 3500 2	C49FT	1986
419	H717DKM	Renault-Dodge 375	Wadham Stringer	B26FL	1991	On extended loan from East Sussex C C
420	H714FUD	Talbot Pullman	TBW Freeway	B16FL	1991	On extended loan from East Sussex C C
421	K927LPO	Mercedes-Benz 709D	Wadham Stringer	B23FL	1993	On extended loan from East Sussex C C
501	E501EFG	Dennis Javelin 12SDA1913	Duple 320	C53FT	1988
502	E502EFG	Dennis Javelin 12SDA1913	Duple 320	C53FT	1988
503	E503EFG	Dennis Javelin 12SDA1913	Duple 320	C53FT	1988
504	F504LAP	Dennis Javelin 12SDA1913	Plaxton Paramount 3200 2	C53FT	1989
505	F505LAP	Dennis Javelin 12SDA1913	Plaxton Paramount 3200 2	C53FT	1989
506	F506LAP	Dennis Javelin 12SDA1913	Plaxton Paramount 3200 2	C53FT	1989
507	G507SAP	Dennis Javelin 12SDA1928	Duple 320	C53FT	1990
508	G508SAP	Dennis Javelin 12SDA1928	Duple 320	C53FT	1990
509	G509SAP	Dennis Javelin 12SDA1928	Duple 320	C53FT	1990

594-603 Bristol VRT/SL3/6LXB Eastern Coach Works CO43/27D 1977 Ex Southdown, 1986

594	TNJ994S	599	TNJ999S	601	TPN101S	602	TPN102S	603	TPN103S

606	UWV606S	Bristol VRT/SL3/6LXB	Eastern Coach Works	CO43/31F 1977	Ex Southdown, 1986
615	UWV615S	Bristol VRT/SL3/6LXB	Eastern Coach Works	CO43/31F 1978	Ex Southdown, 1986
619	UWV619S	Bristol VRT/SL3/6LXB	Eastern Coach Works	CO43/31F 1978	Ex Southdown, 1986

624-633 Bristol VRT/SL3/6LXB Eastern Coach Works H43/27D* 1977 Ex Southdown, 1986
*624 is H43/27F

624	UFG624S	626	UFG626S	628	UFG628S	630	UFG630S	632	UFG632S
625	UFG625S	627	UFG627S	629	UFG629S	631	UFG631S	633	UFG633S

635-651 Bristol VRT/SL3/6LXB Eastern Coach Works H43/31F 1978 Ex Southdown, 1986

635	XAP635S	639	XAP639S	641	XAP641S	645	XAP645S	650	AAP650T
638	XAP638S	640	XAP640S	642	XAP642S	646	AAP646T	651	AAP651T

653-667 Bristol VRT/SL3/6LXB Eastern Coach Works H43/27D 1978-79 Ex Southdown, 1986

653	AAP653T	656	AAP656T	659	AAP659T	665	AAP665T
654	AAP654T	657	AAP657T	663	AAP663T	666	AAP666T
655	AAP655T	658	AAP658T	664	AAP664T	667	AAP667T

674-699 Bristol VRT/SL3/6LXB Eastern Coach Works H43/31F 1979-80 Ex Southdown, 1986

674	EAP974V	676	EAP976V	689	EAP989V	694	EAP994V	698	EAP998V
675	EAP975V	679	EAP979V	693	EAP993V	695	EAP995V	699	EAP999V

701-710 Scania N112DRB East Lancs H47/33F 1988

701	E701EFG	703	E703EFG	705	E705EFG	707	E707EFG	709	E709EFG
702	E702EFG	704	E704EFG	706	E706EFG	708	E708EFG	710	E710EFG

711-730 Scania N113DRB East Lancs H47/33F 1989-90

711	F711LFG	715	F715LFG	719	F719LFG	723	G723RYJ	727	G727RYJ
712	F712LFG	716	F716LFG	720	F720LFG	724	G724RYJ	728	G728RYJ
713	F713LFG	717	F717LFG	721	G721RYJ	725	G725RYJ	729	G729RYJ
714	F714LFG	718	F718LFG	722	G722RYJ	726	G726RYJ	730	G730RYJ

6447	HAP985	Bristol KSW5G	Eastern Coach Works	H32/28R	1953	Ex preservation, 1986

Special liveries
Traditional BH&D livery : 6447
County Rider: 419-21

CHALKWELL COACH HIRE

Chalkwell Garage & Coach Hire Ltd (Chalkwell Coaches), 195 Chalkwell Road, Sittingbourne, Kent

Chalkwell Coach Hire had operated excursions and private hire in the Sittingbourne area for many years before starting local bus operations in April 1990, when Kent County Council contracts were obtained in the Swale area. The fleet has expanded considerably since then, both in terms of coach and bus operation, and the operations of Donsway Coaches, Faversham were acquired in October 1993, together with a number of vehicles. The year 1993 also saw Chalkwell take over local excursion work formerly operated by Maidstone & District from the Medway Towns, and the introduction of commuter services to and from London.
The fleet is operated from Sittingbourne in a livery of white and red with black stripes.

CHALKWELL COACH HIRE

Reg	Chassis	Body	Seating	Year	History
OUP499M	Bedford YRT	Plaxton Elite ExpressIII	C53F	1973	Ex Harris, Dunkirk, 1993
HRR757N	Bedford YRT	Plaxton Elite ExpressIII	C53F	1975	Ex Harris, Dunkirk, 1993
UJP94S	Bedford YMT	Duple Dominant II	C53F	1978	Ex Harris, Dunkirk, 1993
THX235S	Leyland National 10351A/2R		B36D	1978	Ex Harris, Dunkirk, 1993
SJK938S	Bedford YMT	Plaxton Supreme	C49F	1978	Ex Harris, Dunkirk, 1993
YMJ546S	Bedford YMT	Plaxton Supreme	C53F	1978	Ex Harris, Dunkirk, 1993
NSV130	Leyland Leopard PSU5C/4R	Duple Dominant II	C55F	1979	Ex Harris, Dunkirk, 1993
KIW6512	Ford R1114	Plaxton Supreme IV	C53F	1980	Ex Dobsons, Northwich, 1984
PNW315W	Ford R1114	Plaxton Supreme IV	C53F	1981	Ex Wallace Arnold, 1986
TKM108X	Bedford YMT	Wadham Stringer Vanguard	B60F	1982	Ex Happy Days, Woodseaves, 1990
TKM111X	Bedford YMT	Wadham Stringer Vanguard	B60F	1982	Ex Happy Days, Woodseaves, 1990
XPP285X	Leyland Tiger TRCTL11/3R	Plaxton Supreme V	C57F	1982	Ex Cottrell, Mitcheldean, 1992
XPP286X	Leyland Tiger TRCTL11/3R	Plaxton Supreme V	C57F	1982	Ex Cottrell, Mitcheldean, 1993
KIW5235	Leyland Tiger TRCTL11/2R	Plaxton Paramount3200Exp	C53F	1983	Ex Davies, Pencader, 1992
A438NKL	Talbot Express	Rootes	B14FL	1983	Ex Leybourne Grange Hospital, 1990
KIW6419	Leyland Tiger TRCTL11/2R	Plaxton Paramount3200Exp	C53F	1983	Ex Mainwaring, Gilfach Goch, 1990
A211PBM	Ford Transit	Mellor	C16F	1984	Ex Cook & Marshall, Egremont, 1987
KIW7360	Leyland Tiger TRCTL11/2R	Plaxton Paramount 3200	C53F	1984	Ex Mainwaring, Gilfach Goch, 1990
KIW8924	Leyland Tiger TRCTL11/3R	Plaxton Paramount 3500	C53F	1984	Ex Elgar & Fox, Inkpen, 1989
KIW4965	Leyland Tiger TRCTL11/3R	Plaxton Paramount 3200	C53F	1984	Ex Hague, Platts Common, 1993
B501UNB	Leyland Tiger TRCTL11/3RZ	Plaxton Paramount 3500 2	C53F	1985	Ex Filer, Stanton Wick, 1993
C148CGP	Mercedes-Benz L508D	Devon Conversions	C15FL	1985	Ex Kent County Council, 1990
C147CKL	Mercedes-Benz L307D	Robin Hood	C12F	1985	
C552DKE	Ford Transit 190	Chassis Developments	C16F	1985	
D339JUM	Volkswagen LT55	Optare CityPacer	B25F	1986	Ex London Buses, 1992
D344JUM	Volkswagen LT55	Optare CityPacer	B25F	1986	Ex Harris, Dunkirk, 1993
D345JUM	Volkswagen LT55	Optare CityPacer	B25F	1986	Ex London Buses, 1992
D354JUM	Volkswagen LT55	Optare CityPacer	B25F	1986	Ex London Buses, 1992
D355JUM	Volkswagen LT55	Optare CityPacer	B25F	1986	Ex London Buses, 1992
D991WDY	Mercedes-Benz 609D	Pilcher-Greene	B16FL	1987	Ex Sochulbus, Ashford, 1990
D575PKW	Ford Transit 130	Coachcraft	C12F	1987	
D658TKX	Ford Transit 130	Chassis Developments	C12F	1987	Ex Dewberry, Biggin Hill, 1988
E451BFT	Ford Transit	Jubilee	11	1987	Ex van, 1993
E26XKP	Mercedes-Benz L307D	Devon Conversions	C12F	1988	
E360KPO	Iveco Daily 49.10	Robin Hood	C25F	1988	Ex Farnham Coaches, 1988
F106PYR	Ford Transit	Jubilee	16	1988	Ex private owner,1993
F939KKX	Talbot Express	Chassis Developments	C14F	1988	
F749EKM	Mercedes-Benz L307D	Devon Conversions	C12F	1988	
H847DKL	Mercedes-Benz 814	Phoenix	C33F	1990	
H651ENK	DAF 400	Jubilee	C16FL	1991	Ex van, 1993
H46FNK	Iveco Daily 49.10	Dormobile	C16F	1991	Ex demonstrator, 1993
L775CKM	Iveco Daily	Dormobile	B29 F	1994	Ex demonstrator, 1994

Previous registrations

KIW4965	A240ADT	KIW7360	A234GNR
KIW5235	8124DD, PDW275Y	KIW8924	A152RMJ
KIW6419	A379ROU	NSV130	AFH196T
KIW6512	SMB264V		

CHILTERN QUEENS

Chiltern Queens Ltd, Greenmore, Woodcote, Oxfordshire, RG8 0RP

Chiltern Queens was formed in July 1955 as the successor to Kemp's Motor Services Ltd, also of Woodcote. Leyland Leopards and Volvos are now the staple fare with the recent decline of AEC availability. Three main services are operated from Reading together with a town service in Henley-on-Thames and a number of occasional rural services.

CHILTERN QUEENS

Reg	Chassis	Body	Seating	Year	Notes
TUD167G	AEC Reliance 6U3ZR	Plaxton Elite	C57F	1969	
FPX701H	AEC Reliance 6U3ZR	Plaxton Elite	C51F	1970	Ex Byng, Portsmouth, 1972
ABW777J	AEC Reliance 6U3ZR	Plaxton Elite II	C53F	1971	
EUD256K	AEC Reliance 6MU4R	Plaxton Derwent	B47F	1972	
OJO835M	Leyland Leopard PSU3B/4R	Plaxton Derwent	B55F	1974	
VBW581	Leyland Leopard PSU5A/4R	Plaxton Supreme III	C57F	1976	
RFC10T	Leyland Leopard PSU3E/4R	Duple Dominant I Express	C49F	1978	Ex City of Oxford, 1989
RFC12T	Leyland Leopard PSU3E/4R	Duple Dominant I Express	C49F	1978	Ex City of Oxford, 1989
WUD815T	Leyland Leopard PSU3E/4R	Duple Dominant I Express	C49F	1978	Ex City of Oxford, 1989
591STT	Leyland Leopard PSU3E/4R	Plaxton Supreme IV Exp	C53F	1979	
BMO891T	AEC Reliance 6U3ZR	Marshall Camagna	B54F	1979	Ex Ministry of Defence, 1988
YFC18V	Leyland Leopard PSU3E/4R	Duple Dominant II Exp	C49F	1979	Ex City of Oxford, 1991
BBW22V	Leyland Leopard PSU3E/4R	Duple Dominant II Exp	C49F	1979	Ex City of Oxford, 1992
LUA244V	Volvo B58-61	Plaxton Supreme IV	C51F	1980	Ex Parry, Leominster, 1985
MUD25W	Leyland Leopard PSU3F/4R	Duple Dominant II Exp	C53F	1981	Ex City of Oxford, 1993
PJH582X	Leyland Leopard PSU3E/4R	Plaxton Supreme IV	C53F	1982	
B911SPR	Volvo B10M-61	Plaxton Paramount 3200 2	C53F	1985	Ex Excelsior, Bournemouth, 1987
C644SJM	Volvo B10M-61	Plaxton Paramount 3200 2	C53F	1986	
C114PUJ	Volvo B10M-61	Caetano Algarve	C49FT	1986	Ex Hughes, Llanfair Caerelnon, 1993
D262HFX	Volvo B10M-61	Plaxton Paramount 3200 3	C53F	1987	Ex Excelsior, Bournemouth, 1988
E533PRU	Volvo B10M-61	Plaxton Paramount 3200 3	C48FT	1987	
F986TTF	Mercedes-Benz 811D	Optare StarRider	B33F	1987	Ex Lee & Back, Caversham, 1991
F344TSC	Mercedes-Benz 811D	Alexander AM	DP29F	1988	Ex Bowen, Bridgenorth, 1992
H788RWJ	Scania K93CRB	Plaxton Paramount 3200 3	C55F	1990	

Previous registrations
BMO891T	48 AC 82
VBW581	SFC32P
C114PUJ	C690KDS, SEL4X
591STT	UUD623T

A long-time adherent to AECs, Chiltern Queens still muster four Reliances in their fleet. Of these, EUD256K is the only one with pure bus bodywork, in this case by Plaxton, coupled to the increasingly-rare medium-weight chassis with AH505 engine.
Malcolm King

COASTAL COACHES

P.H. Jenkins, 23 Corsica Road, Seaford, East Sussex, BN25 1BD

Coastal Coaches gained an East Sussex County Council contract for service 346 between Silverhill (Hastings) and Pett in October 1990, and two Leyland Nationals were purchased to support this operation. The service has subsequently been extended to the village of Crowhurst and within St Leonards. The vehicles are generally parked at the Silverhill depot of South Coast Buses.

Shown in the last edition with its original registration, Coastal's No.102 in common with its partner now carries a non-year mark. It is seen in Hastings. Terry Blackman

COASTAL COACHES

101	XS2210	Leyland National 10351/1R	DP39F	1976	Ex London Country SW, 1990
102	VY2150	Leyland National 10351A/1R	B41F	1977	Ex East Kent, 1991

Previous registrations
VY2150	PJJ343S
XS2210	LPB189P

EASTBOURNE BUSES

Eastbourne Buses Ltd, Birch Road, Eastbourne, East Sussex, BN23 6PD

Municipal bus operation started in Eastbourne in 1903, being a world first. As a result of deregulation legislation, services are now marketed as Eastbourne Buses. From May 1987 Eastbourne collaborated with Southdown in the Hastings Top Line venture until selling out their share in September 1989.

The once-substantial presence of Leyland Atlanteans in the fleet has almost been eliminated, though some secondhand examples of this type remain in evidence alongside some originals. The Dennis Dominators which succeeded them are now in decline, and Leyland Olympians form the backbone of the double-deck fleet. An increasing number of Dennis single-deckers has been supplemented by two Ikarus Citibuses, and Volvos provide a small coaching element. A notable event in 1993 was the re-acquisition for the 90th anniversary of a vintage AEC Regal.

Fleet colours are biscuit and aircraft blue for buses, while coaches bear biscuit with red and blue, or various tones of bus stripes. All vehicles are accommodated at the Birch Road site.

Below **A delivery of twelve Leyland Olympians with Northern Counties bodywork in 1988 made a radical change in the scene at Eastbourne, and the batch now forms the bulk of the remaining double-deck fleet. No.49 was found on layover in Langney Road, Eastbourne on 8th June 1993.** Paul Gainsbury

Above right **Two long Atlanteans, bodied by East Lancs, survive in the Eastbourne fleet. No.35 was new in 1979 and is seen at the War Memorial roundabout in March 1994.** Paul Gainsbury

Above left **Two Dennis Lances with Wadham Stringer bodywork delivered in 1992 were allocated registrations to reflect the 90th anniversary of the undertaking in 1993. No.14 took letters which form the initials of the Managing Director, and was photographed in Cornfield Road on 26th March 1994.** Paul Gainsbury

The latest generation of Eastbourne open-toppers for the Beachy Head service comprises two Leyland Atlanteans with Eastern Coach Works bodywork purchased from Ipswich in 1990. No.66, painted in distinctive livery and named *Eastbourne King,* stands at the Beachy Head terminus. Malcolm King

An unusual step in 1991 was the purchase of two Leyland Atlanteans with Eastern Coach Works bodies from Colchester. No.29, specially painted in Tilling-style livery, stands at Birch Road on 27th January 1994. Paul Gainsbury

The increasing single-deck presence in Eastbourne results in part from the development of rural routes beyond the town boundary. No.16 is one of two DAF/Ikarus Citibuses delivered in 1994, and is seen at Rye Station Approach on 24th March 1994 at the eastern extremity of operations. Paul Gainsbury

Unusual beasts in the Eastbourne fleet are two Volvos with Duple Dominant bodywork which supplement the Dennises for single-deck work. Acquired from Hutchison, Wishaw in 1992, No.20 dates from 1986 and shows the latest blue-roof livery as it pauses in the town centre. Alan Simpkins

A coaching presence is maintained by four Volvos and a Toyota Coaster. No.4 is one of two Volvo B10Ms with Plaxton coachwork purchased in 1988, and was seen on a market excursion to Rye on 23rd September 1993. Paul Gainsbury

EASTBOURNE BUSES

2	H388CFT	Toyota Coaster HDB30R	Caetano Optimo II	C18F	1991	Ex Ramage, Ferryhill, 1992
3	C580KNO	Volvo B10M-61	Plaxton Paramount 3500 2	C53F	1985	Ex Essex Police, 1991
4	E804DPN	Volvo B10M-61	Plaxton Paramount 3500 3	C53F	1988	
5	E805DPN	Volvo B10M-61	Plaxton Paramount 3500 3	C53F	1988	
6	C347SGD	Volvo B10M-61	Caetano Algarve	C53F	1986	Ex Park, Hamilton, 1989
7	H908DTP	Dennis Dart 9SDL3002	Wadham Stringer PortsdownB35F		1991	Ex Wadham Stringer demonstrator, 1991
8	H840GDY	Dennis Dart 9SDL3002	Wadham Stringer PortsdownB35F		1990	
9	H841GDY	Dennis Dart 9SDL3002	Wadham Stringer PortsdownB35F		1990	
10	G114FJK	Dennis Javelin 11SDL1914	Duple 300	B55F	1990	
11	AHC411	AEC Regal III	East Lancs	DP30R	1950	Ex preservation, 1992
12	G911RPN	Dennis Javelin 11SDL1914	Duple 300	B55F	1989	
13	K90EBL	Dennis Lance 11SDA3101	Wadham Stringer Vanguard II B52F		1992	
14	K90DRH	Dennis Lance 11SDA3101	Wadham Stringer Vanguard II B52F		1992	
15	K315MWV	Dennis Lance 11SDA3101	Wadham Stringer Vanguard II B52F		1993	
16	L416UNJ	DAF SB220LC550	Ikarus Citibus	B48F	1994	
17	L417UUF	DAF SB220LC550	Ikarus Citibus	B48F	1994	
19	D499NYS	Volvo B10M-61	Duple Dominant	B55F	1986	Ex Hutchison, Wishaw, 1992
20	D497NYS	Volvo B10M-61	Duple Dominant	B55F	1986	Ex Hutchison, Wishaw, 1992
21	J221FUF	Dennis Dart 9.8SDL3012	Wadham Stringer PortsdownB43F		1991	
22	J122FUF	Dennis Dart 9.8SDL3012	Wadham Stringer PortsdownB43F		1992	
23	J223FUF	Dennis Javelin 11SDL1924	Wadham Stringer Vanguard II B55F		1992	
24	J124FUF	Dennis Javelin 11SDL1924	Wadham Stringer Vanguard II B55F		1991	
25	G25HDW	Dennis Javelin 11SDL1907	Duple 300	B55F	1990	Ex Bebb, Llantwit Fardre, 1991
26	G28HDW	Dennis Javelin 11SDL1907	Duple 300	B55F	1990	Ex Bebb, Llantwit Fardre, 1991
27	J127LHC	Dennis Javelin 11SDL1924	Plaxton Derwent II	DP53F	1991	
29	NNO62P	Leyland Atlantean AN68A/1R	Eastern Coach Works	H43/31F	1975	Ex Colchester, 1991
34	YJK934V	Leyland Atlantean AN68A/2R	East Lancs	H47/35F	1979	
35	YJK935V	Leyland Atlantean AN68A/2R	East Lancs	H47/35F	1979	
38	MPN138W	Dennis Dominator DD120	East Lancs	H43/31F	1981	
39	MPN139W	Dennis Dominator DD120	East Lancs	H43/31F	1981	

42-46

		Dennis Dominator DDA154	East Lancs	H43/31F	1982	

42	FDY142X	43	FDY143X	44	FDY144X	45	FDY145X	46	FDY146X

47-58

		Leyland Olympian ONCL10/2RZ	Northern Counties	H47/30F	1988

47	E847DPN	50	E850DPN	53	E853DPN	56	E856DPN
48	E848DPN	51	E851DPN	54	E854DPN	57	E857DPN
49	E849DPN	52	E852DPN	55	E855DPN	58	E858DPN

64	NNO64P	Leyland Atlantean AN68A/1R	Eastern Coach Works	H43/31F	1975	Ex Colchester, 1991
65	LDX75G	Leyland Atlantean PDR1/1	Eastern Coach Works	O43/31F	1968	Ex Ipswich, 1990
66	LDX76G	Leyland Atlantean PDR1/1	Eastern Coach Works	O43/31F	1968	Ex Ipswich, 1990
67	JWF47W	Leyland Atlantean AN68/1R	Roe	H43/29F	1980	Ex London Cityrama, London SW8, 1994
68	JVF315S	Leyland Atlantean AN68/2R	East Lancs	H50/36F	1988	Ex Blackpool, 1994
69	JVF316S	Leyland Atlantean AN68/2R	East Lancs	H50/36F	1988	Ex Blackpool, 1994
82	DHC782E	Leyland Titan PD2A/30	East Lancs	H32/28R	1967	

Named vehicles
65 Eastbourne Queen, 66 Eastbourne King

Special liveries
Overall advertisements : 17, 21, 42, 54/7/8
Traditional livery : 11

EASTONWAYS

E.L. & Y.M. Easton (Eastonways), 12 Montefiore Avenue, Ramsgate, Kent

Eastonways has developed substantially in the past few years. From a fleet of three coaches engaged in contract and private hire work, a small group of local bus services was built up on the Isle of Thanet from 1991, including some operated within Kent County Council's 'Kent Karrier' scheme; more recently, Eastonways have expanded with operations to and from the developing Port Ramsgate complex, for which a large number of second-hand vehicles have been acquired.

The main fleet livery is white and blue, though several vehicles operate in as-acquired colours.

EASTONWAYS

2	OJD903R	Leyland National 10351A/2R		B36D	1977	Ex Port Ramsgate (npsv), 1994
3	OJD893R	Leyland National 10351A/2R		B36D	1977	Ex Port Ramsgate (npsv), 1994
4	KJD549P	Leyland National 10351A/2R		B36D	1976	Ex Port Ramsgate (npsv), 1994
5	THX146S	Leyland National 10351A/2R		B36D	1978	Ex Warren, Ticehurst, 1994
6	THX246S	Leyland National 10351A/2R		B36D	1978	Ex Vanguard, Bedworth, 1994
7	VKE569S	Leyland National 11351A/1R		B49F	1977	Ex Roffey, Flimwell, 1994
8	BYW372V	Leyland National 10351A/2R		B36D	1979	Ex Evag Cannon, Bolton, 1994
11	BYW376V	Leyland National 10351A/2R		B24D	1979	Ex Port Ramsgate (npsv), 1994
15	WFM803L	Leyland National 1151/2R/0401		B17D	1972	Ex Port Ramsgate (npsv), 1994
	EUI1586	Leyland Leopard PSU3B/4R	Plaxton Panorama Elite III	C51F	1973	Ex Kemp, Chillenden, 1989
	GBZ7129	Leyland Leopard PSU3B/4R	Duple Dominant	C51F	1974	Ex Fylde, 1991
	THM614M	Daimler Fleetline CRL6	MCW	H44/28D	1974	Ex New Enterprise, Chatham, 1993
	VOR813N	Bedford YRQ	Plaxton Elite Express III	C45F	1974	Ex Kemp, Chillenden, 1993
	976NE	Leyland Leopard PSU3C/4R	Plaxton Supreme Express	C53F	1976	Ex Wealden, Five Oak Green, 1992
	EUI1587	Leyland Leopard PSU3C/4R	Duple Dominant I	C53F	1977	Ex Montgomery, Bromley, 1992
	OJV118S	Leyland Fleetline FE30AGR	Roe	H45/29D	1977	Ex Wealden PSV, Five Oak Green, 1994
	GBZ7128	Leyland Leopard PSU3E/4R	Duple Dominant II	C53F	1978	Ex Kemp, Chillenden, 1991
	WCK142V	Leyland Leopard PSU3E/4R	Duple Dominant II Express	C49F	1980	Ex Midland Red North, 1994
	JNM754Y	Mercedes-Benz L508DG	Reeve Burgess	C19F	1983	Ex G. Stone, Aldershot, 1994
	A161TGE	MCW Metroliner DR130/4	MCW	CH53/16DT	1984	Ex Mancunian, Bradford, 1994
	A690CJR	Ford Transit	Ford	C16F	1984	Ex private owner, 1994
	C449SJU	Ford Transit VE6	Robin Hood City Nippy	B16F	1985	Ex Lea, Emsworth, 1991
	D50KAX	Iveco Daily 49.10	Robin Hood City Nippy	B21F	1986	Ex McCarthey, Stalybridge, 1994
	D611BCK	Iveco Daily 49.10	Robin Hood City Nippy	B21F	1987	Ex Ribble, 1993
	D39DNH	Iveco Daily 49.10	Robin Hood City Nippy	B19F	1987	Ex United Counties, 1993
	F726EKR	Ford Transit VE6	Dormobile	C16F	1988	
	G645EVN	CVE Omni	CVE	B23F	1990	Ex East Kent, 1992
	J110LKO	OBC Omni	OBC	B20F	1991	Ex Kent County Council, 1993
	J998LKR	OBC Omni	OBC	DP21F	1991	

Previous registrations

EUI1586	KBU895L	GBZ7129	YNA398M
EUI1587	SAD121R	976NE	NEL115P
GBZ7128	VYK201S		

Named vehicles
EUI1586 Duchess of Kent, EUI1587 Maid of Kent, GBZ7128 Princess of Kent

EAST SURREY

East Surrey Buses, Lambs Business Park, Tilburstow Hill, South Godstone, Surrey, RH9 8JZ

East Surrey Buses have developed a higher profile in local bus work since deregulation, and in recent times have gained some significant contracts from both Kent and Surrey County Councils, in addition to expanding commercial initiatives. Most recently a group of services in the Sevenoaks area was gained from April 1994, and the network extends into Tunbridge Wells through co-ordinated operation of tendered routes with Wealden-Beeline.

The original fleet, largely based on Bedford chassis, has been updated with Optare StarRiders, two Optare MetroRiders, Omnis and Dennis Darts. Some coaches are also held for private hire work.

Fleet livery is orange and cream, and the vehicles are based at South Godstone.

The 1992 round of Kent County Council tendering at Tunbridge Wells brought East Surrey onto the East Grinstead corridor as sub-contractors to Wealden-Beeline. Dennis Dart 36 had served as a Wadham Stringer demonstrator before being acquired late in 1991, and was seen at the eastern end of the route in July 1993. Terry Blackman

One of three Dennis Darts with Plaxton 'Pointer' bodywork delivered in 1993, No.45 pauses as it leaves Benhall Mill Road, Tunbridge Wells on local route 285 which was gained in the spring 1994 round of Kent County Council tenders. David Harman

EAST SURREY

No.	Reg	Chassis	Body	Seating	Year	Notes
8	TAA744T	Bedford YMT	Plaxton Supreme III	C53F	1979	Ex Taylor, Caterham, 1986
10	GPA620V	Bedford YMT	Duple Dominant II	C53F	1980	Ex Porter, Dunmer, 1986
18	E318SYG	Mercedes-Benz 811D	Optare StarRider	B33F	1988	
19	MPE248P	Bedford YRQ	Plaxton Derwent	B49F	1976	Ex Farnham Coaches, 1988
20	VDL264K	Bedford YRQ	Plaxton Derwent	B49F	1972	Ex Gale, Haslemere, 1988
24	F70RPL	Mercedes-Benz 811D	Optare StarRider	DP33F	1989	
25	G301CPL	Mercedes-Benz 811D	Optare StarRider	B33F	1989	
26	G972WPA	Optare Metrorider	Optare	B33F	1990	
27	UGB14R	AEC Reliance 6U3ZR	Duple Dominant	B53F	1977	Ex Moss, Sandown, 1990
29	H743LHN	CVE Omni	CVE	B23F	1990	
30	H744LHN	CVE Omni	CVE	B21FL	1990	
31	H745LHN	CVE Omni	CVE	B21FL	1990	
32	OHV208Y	Ford R1114	Wadham Stringer Vanguard	B33F	1982	Ex London Borough of Lewisham, 1991
33	YLN636S	Ford R1014	Duple Dominant	B47F	1978	Ex London Borough of Hillingdon, 1991
34	J326PPD	Optare Metrorider	Optare	B33F	1991	
35	VNU533Y	Ford R1014	Duple Dominant	B47F	1982	Ex Lamcote, Radcliffe, 1991
36	J752PPM	Dennis Dart 9SDL3002	Wadham Stringer Portsdown	B37F	1991	Ex demonstrator, 1991
37	D602RGJ	Bedford YMT	Plaxton Derwent	B53F	1987	Ex Epsom Buses, 1991
38	D167TAU	Bedford YMT	Duple Dominant	B55F	1986	Ex National Plant, South Normanton, 1992
39	KHF933P	Bedford YRQ	Plaxton Supreme	DP45F	1975	Ex Pulham, Bourton, 1992
40	B88BVW	Ford R1015	Wadham Stringer Vanguard	B33F	1985	Ex Wealden, Five Oak Green, 1992
41	C915BYP	Bedford YMP	Wadham Stringer Vanguard	DP45F	1985	Ex Civil Service College, 1992
42	D380BNR	Bedford YNT	Plaxton Paramount 3500 3	C57F	1987	Ex Owen, Tayeley, 1992
43	RET150M	Bedford YRT	Plaxton	C53F	1974	Ex Gagg, Bunny, 1992
44	K467TKJ	OBC Omni	OBC	B20FL	1993	
45	K488XPG	Dennis Dart 9.8SDL3017	Plaxton Pointer	B40F	1993	
46	E132PLJ	Dennis Javelin 12SDA1907	Plaxton Paramount 3200 3	C53F	1988	Ex Taylor, Sutton Scotney, 1993
47	L726DPG	Dennis Dart 9.8SDL3035	Plaxton Pointer	B40F	1993	
48	L735MWW	Optare Metrorider	Optare	B29F	1993	
49	L354FPF	Dennis Dart	Plaxton Pointer	B40F	1994	

FARLEIGH COACHES

D.R. Smith, St Peter's Works, Hall Road, Wouldham, Kent, ME1 3XL

Farleigh Coaches commenced local coaching operations in August 1982, though not using this trading name until later. Bus operations were introduced at deregulation and although a weekday evening contract between Maidstone and Borough Green has since passed elsewhere, the main service 58 between Maidstone and Trottiscliffe remains. This is notable in having been introduced commercially to replace a Maidstone & District facility, although it is now provided as a Kent County Council contract. The usual vehicle is now a former London Buses Leyland National, with a former East Kent AEC Swift as the first reserve.

Fleet livery is white with red lettering.

FARLEIGH COACHES

VJG187J	AEC Swift 5P2R	Marshall	B51F	1970	Ex Blue Birds Majorettes, Maidstone, 1987
WFS228K	Leyland Atlantean PDR1A/1	Alexander J	H45/33F	1972	Ex Ulsterbus, 1990
JGF410K	Daimler Fleetline CRL6	Park Royal	H44/29F	1972	Ex Tellyn, Little Baddow, 1983
VPB123M	Leyland Atlantean AN68/1R	Park Royal	H43/28D	1974	Ex Turner, West Farleigh, 1993
NOE591R	Leyland National 11351A/1R		B49F	1977	Ex Muttiff, Morley, 1992
THX140S	Leyland National 10351A/2R		B36D	1977	Ex London Buses, 1991
BTH364V	AEC Reliance 6U3ZR	Duple Dominant II Express	C53F	1979	Ex Steel, Addingham, 1991
SIB3059	AEC Reliance 6U3ZR	Van Hool Aragon	C53F	1979	Ex Horlock, Northfleet, 1991
PVV314	DAF MB200DKTL600	Caetano Alpha GT	C53F	1983	Ex Street, Dickington, 1993
A114KBA	MCW Metroliner DR130/2	MCW	CH55/18CT	1984	Ex Ward, Harlow, 1993
A332PNW	DAF SB2300DHTD585	Plaxton Paramount 3200	C53F	1984	Ex Hallums, Southend, 1993
B826AAT	MCW Metroliner DR130/3	MCW	CH57/18F	1984	Ex Pride of the Road, Royston, 1993
SIB3058	DAF SB2300DHS585	Jonckheere Bermuda	C51FT	1985	Ex Gillespie, Kelty, 1992
SIB3057	DAF SB2305DHS585	Caetano Algarve	C53F	1989	
WOI4006	Ward Dalesman TV8-640	Van Hool Alizée	C49FT	1983	Ex Prentice & McQuillan, Swanley, 1994

Previous registrations

PVV314	CAY215Y	SIB3059	NMJ291V		
SIB3057	F438RRY	WOI4006	GCP789Y		
SIB3058	B496GB	B826AAT	B118ORU, A4GNT		

One of two Leyland Nationals which normally support KCC service 58, NOE591R started life with Midland Red, arriving with Farleigh Coaches in 1992 from another independent. David Harman

FUGGLES

Fuggles of Benenden Ltd, Bramley Orchard, Cranbrook Road, Benenden, Kent, TN17 4EU

Fuggles traces its origins back to the late 1920s and the establishment of a garage in the country village in 1927. The firm passed into new management during the summer of 1989 and the original trading name was reinstated after a period during which the limited company name of Penjon had been used for official purposes.

Stage services started in June 1980 and the company subsequently built up a network of services in the rural area bordered by Maidstone, Tunbridge Wells and Tenterden. Many of these were operated on a commercial basis. The recession has meant that most of them have since come under Kent County Council auspices, and some have been lost to other operators. However, a Kent Karrier service was gained in the Ashford area in 1992, and there is also Saturday work on East Sussex County Council route 312 from Tenterden to Rye.

Fleet livery is deep red and cream with pale red relief, and the fleet is housed in a new depot at Apple Pie Farm, Benenden.

FUGGLES

10	L10FUG	Dennis Dart 9.8SDL3032	Wadham Stringer Portsdown	B43F	1994	
	AKM425K	Leyland Leopard PSU4A/2R	Willowbrook	B52F	1971	Ex Wealden, Five Oak Green, 1990
	STD119L	Leyland Leopard PSU4B/2R	Seddon Pennine	B47F	1972	Ex Maidstone Borough Council, 1982
	LUG523P	Leyland Leopard PSU4C/4R	Plaxton Derwent	B52F	1976	Ex Wealden, Five Oak Green, 1992
	RAW29R	Bedford YLQ	Duple Dominant II	C45F	1977	Ex Morgan, Ingatestone, 1990
	PBO674R	Leyland Leopard PSU4D/2R	Plaxton Derwent	B53F	1977	Ex Red & White, 1993
	SKN910R	Leyland National 11351A/1R		DP48F	1977	Ex Hastings & District, 1989
	SKN911R	Leyland National 11351A/1R		DP46F	1977	Ex Hastings & District, 1989
	UFT911T	Bedford YLQ	Plaxton Supreme III	C45F	1978	Ex Rowland & Goodwin, St Leonard's, 1983
	APH529T	Bedford YMT	Plaxton Supreme IV	C53F	1979	Ex Lock, London SE8, 1993
	HVC10V	Bedford YMT	Plaxton Supreme IV	C53F	1979	Ex Rowland & Goodwin, St Leonard's, 1984
	BTE205V	Leyland Leopard PSU3E/4RT	Duple Dominant II Express	C53F	1980	Ex Nazir, Aylesbury, 1993
	NKY275X	Mercedes-Benz L207D	Whittaker	C12F	1982	Ex Goulding, Knottingley, 1987
	BUT47Y	Bedford YNT	Plaxton Paramount 3200Exp	C53F	1983	Ex Wainfleet, Nuneaton, 1987
	A76JFA	Leyland Tiger TRCTL11/3RH	Plaxton Paramount 3200Exp	C53F	1984	Ex Harrison & Brunt, Derby, 1994
	B420CMC	Mercedes-Benz L608D	Reeve Burgess	C21F	1985	Ex Garcia, London W2, 1989
	J996MKM	OBC Omni	OBC	DP21F	1991	Ex Wealden, Five Oak Green, 1992
	L822PEG	Ford Transit	Dormobile	DP18FL	1994	Ex Kent County Council, 1994

A surprise move in 1989 was the arrival with Fuggles of two Leyland Nationals with dual-purpose seating from Hastings & District in exchange for Bristol REs (one of which subsequently passed to Bexhill Bus and is depicted elsewhere in this book). SKN911R arrives in Rye on the route from Tenterden. Terry Blackman

GREY-GREEN

T Cowie, Maritime Way, Medway City Estate, Frindsbury, Strood, Kent

A new depot for Medway operations was opened in Strood in September 1988. Largely servicing commuter coach services to and from London, this has also been used as a foothold for Kent County Council contracts, which currently comprise routes in the Medway Towns and a longer-distance group of routes from Chatham via Maidstone and West Malling to Tonbridge and Tunbridge Wells. The operations of Allways, Sittingbourne were taken over on 29th March 1992.

Local bus work is provided by three Leyland Lynxes acquired from Merthyr Tydfil and five Leyland Nationals from County Bus, whilst coaches are drawn from the main London fleet. Buses are painted in a livery of grey and green with orange and white relief, whilst coaches are in white with orange and green stripes.

GREY-GREEN Vehicles based at Strood

101	B101XYH	Auwaerter Neoplan N122/3	Plaxton Paramount 4000	CH55/20DT	1984	
102	B102XYH	Auwaerter Neoplan N122/3	Plaxton Paramount 4000	CH55/20DT	1985	
103	C103CYE	Scania K112TRS	Plaxton Paramount 4000 2	CH57/18CT	1985	
801	D101NDW	Leyland Lynx LX112TL11ZR1R	Leyland	B51F	1987	Ex Merthyr Tydfil, 1989
802	D102NDW	Leyland Lynx LX112TL11ZR1R	Leyland	B51F	1987	Ex Merthyr Tydfil, 1989
803	D108NDW	Leyland Lynx LX112TL11ZR1R	Leyland	B51F	1987	Ex Merthyr Tydfil, 1989
804	LPB203P	Leyland National 10351/1R		B41F	1976	Ex County, 1992
805	LPB211P	Leyland National 10351/1R		B41F	1976	Ex County, 1992
806	NPK229R	Leyland National 10351A/1R		B41F	1976	Ex County, 1992
807	SPC265R	Leyland National 10351A/1R		B41F	1977	Ex County, 1992
808	UPB296S	Leyland National 10351A/1R		B41F	1977	Ex County, 1992
875	C875CYX	Volvo B10M-61	Plaxton Paramount 3200 2	C53F	1986	
877	C877CYX	Volvo B10M-61	Plaxton Paramount 3200 2	C53F	1986	
880	D880FYL	Volvo B10M-61	Plaxton Paramount 3200 3	C53F	1987	
881	D881FYL	Volvo B10M-61	Plaxton Paramount 3200 3	C53F	1987	
882	D882FYL	Volvo B10M-61	Plaxton Paramount 3500 3	C49FT	1987	
883	D883FYL	Volvo B10M-61	Plaxton Paramount 3500 3	C49FT	1987	
884	D884FYL	Volvo B10M-61	Plaxton Paramount 3500 3	C49FT	1987	
885	E885KYW	Leyland Lynx LX112TL11ZR1	Leyland	B47F	1987	
886	E886KYW	Leyland Lynx LX112TL11ZR1	Leyland	B47F	1987	
895	E895KYW	Scania K92CRB	Van Hool Alizée	C53F	1988	
896	E896KYW	Scania K92CRB	Van Hool Alizée	C53F	1988	
897	E897KYW	Scania K92CRB	Van Hool Alizée	C53F	1988	
898	E898KYW	Scania K92CRB	Van Hool Alizée	C53F	1988	
901	E901MUC	Volvo B10M-61	Van Hool Alizée	C49FT	1988	
902	E902MUC	Volvo B10M-61	Van Hool Alizée	C49FT	1988	
903	E903MUC	Volvo B10M-61	Van Hool Alizée	C49FT	1988	

Further KCC gains during 1992 led to Grey-Green buying five Leyland Nationals from County Bus. No.807 takes layover in Military Road, Chatham before heading (though apparently without due public notice) towards West Malling. Malcolm King

HANTS & SUSSEX

B.S. Williams Ltd, Hollybank House, Emsworth, Hampshire, PO10 7LN

The original Hants & Sussex Motor Services Ltd had a chequered history between its formation in 1907 and cessation in 1954. The proprietor, Mr Basil Williams, formed a new company in his own name in October 1955, purchasing Glider & Blue Motor Services Ltd of Bishops Waltham and Fareham in December 1959. In 1962 the fleetname Southern Motorways was adopted. The coach interests of White Heather Transport Ltd, Southsea were acquired in 1977 and a new company, White Heather Travel, was formed on 1st October of that year to take over the fleet of seven coaches. Victoria Coaches, Southsea was a further acquisition in May 1979. White Heather was sold in June 1984, and the Glider & Blue section was sold to Solent Blue Line on 1st October 1987.

The residual services fall into two groups, centred on Emsworth and Midhurst. Vehicles carry a livery of red, cream and black (coaches are cream and red) and are based at Southleigh Farm, Southleigh Road, Emsworth.

HANTS & SUSSEX

VLW217G	AEC Merlin 4P2R	MCW	B41D	1968	Ex Mobil Oil, Coryton, 1989
VLW529G	AEC Merlin 4P2R	MCW	B50F	1969	Ex Clifton College, Bristol, 1989
AML97H	AEC Swift 4MP2R	Park Royal	B32D	1969	Ex P&O, Dover, 1989
AML567H	AEC Merlin 4P2R	MCW	B50F	1969	Ex P&O, Dover, 1989
AML570H	AEC Merlin 4P2R	MCW	B47F	1969	Ex Harris, Dunkirk, 1990
AML601H	AEC Merlin 4P2R	MCW	B50F	1969	Ex Buckland & Hetherington, 1992
AML605H	AEC Merlin 4P2R	MCW	B—D	1969	Ex Time, Thornton Heath, 1993
BPH114H	AEC Swift 4MP2R	Park Royal	B43F	1970	Ex London Country, 1985
BPH144H	AEC Swift 4MP2R	Park Royal	B43F	1970	Ex Glider & Blue, Emsworth, 1989
DPD502J	AEC Swift 4MP2R/1	MCW	B43D	1971	Ex Gatwick Handling, Gatwick, 1986
EGN683J	AEC Swift 4MP2R/3	MCW	B43F	1971	Ex preservation, 1988
KKW66P	Leyland Leopard PSU3C/4R	Alexander AY	DP49F	1976	Ex West Riding, 1990
PJI4982	Leyland Leopard PSU5A/4R	Plaxton Supreme III	C50F	1976	Ex Hallum, Southend, 1991
135MHT	Leyland Leopard PSU3E/4R	Plaxton Supreme IV	C53F	1978	Ex Shamrock & Rambler, 1988
WRO434S	Leyland Leopard PSU3E/4R	Duple Dominant II	C53F	1978	Ex Southend, 1988
CTM406T	Leyland Leopard PSU3E/4R	Duple Dominant II	C53F	1979	Ex Southend, 1988
CTM407T	Leyland Leopard PSU3E/4R	Duple Dominant II	C53F	1979	Ex Southend, 1988
L625RPX	Iveco Daily 59.12	European Coach Conversions	B29F	1993	

Previous registrations

PJI4982	NUR82P
135MHT	WOC729T

Hants & Sussex have for several years been identified with ex-London AEC Merlins and Swifts, though these are now in gradual decline. The oldest, VLW217G, had spent twelve years in use for experimental and less-refined purposes in London before passing into independent ownership, arriving with Hants & Sussex in 1989. Malcolm McDonald

KENT COACH TOURS

D.C. Farmer, 98 Ellingham Way, Ashford, Kent, TN23 2NF

From October 1986 Kent Coach Tours secured a Kent County Council contract between Ashford and Faversham, with some journeys extended to Oare and Luddenham. In March 1988 a local Ashford service was added, followed by a service from Folkestone to Dover through the Alkham Valley in April 1990. A further local service in the Ashford area was introduced commercially in November 1990. Having lost the Faversham service in March 1992 and with a possibility of losing the tendered local Ashford route, Kent Coach Tours registered the latter commercially and introduced an enhanced timetable coupling it to the existing commercial service. Some rationalisation of services with East Kent took place in November 1992, and the Faversham route was regained when Westbus withdrew from their KCC commitments in October 1993.
Most of the fleet operates in a two-tone blue livery.

KENT COACH TOURS

KDW333P	Leyland National 11351/1R		B49F	1975	Ex Westbus, Ashford, 1993
MUA869P	Leyland Atlantean AN68/1R	Park Royal/Roe	H43/30F	1976	Ex Hulme Hall, Cheadle Hulme, 1993
NFN85R	Leyland National 11351A/1R		DP48F	1977	Ex Warren, Ticehurst, 1993
OJD890R	Leyland National 10351A/2R		B36D	1977	Ex Bailey, Folkestone, 1994
UUR349W	Leyland Leopard PSU5C/4R	Plaxton Supreme IV	C57F	1981	Ex Chambers, Stevenage, 1991
EBD181X	Leyland Leopard PSU3G/4RT	Eastern Coach Works B51	C49F	1982	Ex Hill, Congleton, 1990
LAG313Y	Leyland Tiger TRCTL11/3R	Plaxton Paramount 3500	C50F	1983	Ex Dorset Travel Services, 1991
KCT638	Leyland Tiger TRCTL11/3R	Plaxton Paramount 3500	C48FT	1983	Ex Dorset Travel Services, 1991
A41SKL	Ford R1115	Plaxton Paramount 3200Exp	C53F	1983	Ex Andrews, Trudoxhill, 1989
KCT415	DAF SB2300DHS585	Plaxton Paramount 3500	C53FT	1984	Ex Kelly & Meek, Cheltenham, 1992
KCT986	Bova FHD12-280	Bova Futura	C49FT	1985	Ex D Truelove, Liversedge, 1988
E464ANC	Mercedes-Benz 609D	Made to Measure	C25F	1988	Ex Ratcliffe, Oswaldtwistle, 1992
G846MKY	Mercedes-Benz 609D	Whittaker	B24F	1990	Ex Brown, Builth Wells, 1994
K13KCT	Mercedes-Benz 814D	Plaxton	DP33F	1993	

Previous registrations

KCT415	A261BTY	LAG313Y	GRH2Y
KCT638	EWW951Y	A41SKL	A56HAD, KCT638
KCT986	B556KRY		

Named vehicles
LAG313Y Kent Cruiser, A41SKL Somerset Cruiser

LEISURELINK

Abacus Carriage Services Ltd, PO Box 333, Crawley, West Sussex, RH10 2YT

Leisurelink operates a small fleet of open-top vehicles for private hire and leisure services in Surrey and Sussex. During the summer of 1994 they are involved in Surrey County Council Sunday service 88 (Horsted Keynes to Gatwick Airport) and 439 (Gatwick Airport to Leatherhead).

LEISURELINK

VLT120	AEC Routemaster	Park Royal	O36/28R	1959	Ex London Bus Preservation Group, 1993
ADV299A	Leyland Atlantean PDR1/1	Metro-Cammell	O44/31F	1961	Ex North Devon, 1993
AOR157B	Leyland Titan PD3/4	Northern Counties	FO39/30F	1964	Ex Southdown, 1992
BUF429C	Leyland Titan PD3/4	Northern Counties	FCO39/30F	1965	Ex Powell, Merthyr Tydfil, 1992

Previous registrations

ADV299A	925GTA	AOR157B	422DCD

36

After suffering a number of tendering losses, Kent Coach Tours has been a beneficiary of recent awards, including some occasioned by the premature withdrawal of incumbent operators. Former East Kent Leyland National NFN85R arrived from Warren, Ticehurst in the autumn of 1993 in time for re-acquisition of the Ashford to Faversham service, being found in Faversham.

One of the former Devon General 'Sea Dog' Atlanteans now owned by Leisurelink, 928GTA has a convertible open-top Metro-Cammell body. On 10th April 1994 it was seen working a special service for the Cobham Bus Rally at Weybridge. Ivor Norman

MAIDSTONE & DISTRICT

The Maidstone & District Motor Services Ltd, Luton Road, Chatham, Kent, ME5 7LH

Maidstone & District was formed in 1911 and at one time held sway throughout the western half of Kent and into East Sussex. Today its operations are rather more compact, taking in the Medway Towns, Maidstone, Tonbridge, Tunbridge Wells and the Swale area, together with a presence in the Weald of Kent. There is a strong London commuter service from the Medway Towns and Maidstone, marketed under the 'Invictaway' banner.

Maidstone & District was one of the first National Bus Company subsidiaries to be privatised when it was sold to a management team on 6th November 1986, through Einkorn Ltd, an off-the-shelf company. In June 1988 the competing New Enterprise Coaches of Tonbridge was bought out; this operation continues as an Einkorn subsidiary and now concentrates on school, excursion and private hire work. The residual vehicles of Boro'line Maidstone were purchased on 12th June 1992 (though all were quickly sold), together with their Maidstone depot, and from 29th May 1994 M&D have taken over the bus operations of Bygone Buses in the Maidstone area after three and a half years of at times difficult competition.

Fleet livery is grass green with cream relief. Coaches and Invictaway vehicles carry schemes derived from the old National Bus Company using these colours. The fleet operates from garages at Edenbridge, Gillingham, Hawkhurst, Luton (Chatham), Maidstone and Tunbridge Wells, together with open outstations at Sheerness, Sittingbourne and Tenterden. The New Enterprise fleet has its own site in Tonbridge.

The first Volvo B6s in the area are ten delivered to Maidstone & District with Plaxton bodywork in the spring of 1994. This view of No.3607 in Tunbridge Wells shows the livery style for this batch, together with the first use of Dayglo blinds by M&D. David Harman

M&D bought ten MCW Metrobus Mk2 double-deckers in 1984, though these were to remain unique in the fleet. All are now based at Luton (Chatham), whence No.5203 was operating when found at the north-west corner of the M&D area in Gravesend on 29th April 1994. *Gerald Mead*

In 1984 M&D purchased three Leyland Olympians with Eastern Coach Works coach-seated bodywork which were no longer required for a Devon General order. No.5890 in Maidstone shows a regular haunt of these vehicles on the long trunk route to Hastings. *Terry Blackman*

The need to increase the double-deck fleet at the end of 1991 for expanded services in Maidstone led M&D to buy Leyland Atlanteans from Luton & District. No.5739, one of four with Roe bodywork, loads in High Street at Maidstone on one of the services which until the early 1990s had been the province of Boro'line Maidstone.
John Grubb

The fourteen Leyland Olympians with Eastern Coach Works coach-seated bodies originally used on Invictaway work have now been cascaded to bus duty or sold. No.5443 is one of five to have received a special livery for use on the Maidstone to Gillingham route, on which it was found in Chatham on 13th June 1994.
Gerald Mead

The acquisition of the local routes of the Shearings group at the end on 1991 brought four Leyland Lynxes into the M&D fleet. In mid-1992 these were repainted into Maidstone Park-and-Ride livery when the Coombe Quarry to London Road service was taken over from Boro'line Maidstone. No.3046 stands at the Coombe Quarry terminus.
Terry Blackman

40

Dennis Dominators have formed a significant element of the Medway-based fleet, though withdrawal is now in hand. No.5302, bodied by Willowbrook, is the oldest survivor of only six that were actually new to the company, the rest having arrived from other sources. This view at Military Road, Chatham on 15th July 1993 has wrapround advertising for a local shopping centre. John Grubb

The current standard double-deck is the Olympian with Northern Counties bodywork. No.5907, new in 1993, was amongst the last to bear the Leyland marque, and was photographed still in pristine condition at Queen's Monument, Maidstone in February 1993. Terry Blackman

In the early days of the series 3 Bristol VRT, M&D conducted evaluation trials for the National Bus Company with four such vehicles against Volvo Ailsas and Scania Metropolitans. No.5105, one of the vehicles involved in these trials, is now the oldest VRT in the fleet, and spends its life on rural routes in the Weald of Kent. This view shows it at Tenterden (Vine). Nicholas King

M&D is unusual in that the first generation of minibuses remains intact. No.1027 is one of a batch of 39 Mercedes-Benz L608Ds with locally-converted Rootes bodywork delivered in 1986, and was found at Tunbridge Wells Sainsbury's on a recently-converted local route on 11th September 1993.
Nicholas King

Amongst five Leyland Tigers purchased second-hand by M&D at the end of 1993 were three with Plaxton '321' bodywork. No.2196 came from Bebb, Llantwit Fardre and was photographed showing the current version of Invictaway livery in the spring of 1994.
Richard Lewis

MAIDSTONE & DISTRICT

| 1000 | C203PCD | Mercedes-Benz L608D | Alexander AM | B20F | 1986 | Ex Brighton & Hove, 1990 |

| *1001-1039* | | Mercedes-Benz L608D | Rootes | B20F | 1986 |

1001	C201EKJ	1009	C209EKJ	1017	C217EKJ	1025	D25KKP	1033	D33KKP
1002	C202EKJ	1010	C210EKJ	1018	C218EKJ	1026	D26KKP	1034	D34KKP
1003	C203EKJ	1011	C211EKJ	1019	C219EKJ	1027	D27KKP	1035	D35KKP
1004	C204EKJ	1012	C212EKJ	1020	C220EKJ	1028	D28KKP	1036	D36KKP
1005	C205EKJ	1013	C213EKJ	1021	C221EKJ	1029	D29KKP	1037	D37KKP
1006	C206EKJ	1014	C214EKJ	1022	D22KKP	1030	D30KKP	1038	D38KKP
1007	C207EKJ	1015	C215EKJ	1023	D23KKP	1031	D31KKP	1039	D39KKP
1008	C208EKJ	1016	C216EKJ	1024	D24KKP	1032	D32KKP		

| 1040 | D441RKE | Mercedes-Benz 609D | Reeve Burgess | B20F | 1987 | Ex Marinair, Canterbury, 1988 |

| *1041-1087* | | Mercedes-Benz 609D | Reeve Burgess | B20F* | 1987-90 | * 1077/8 are DP19F |

1041	E41UKL	1051	E51UKL	1061	E61UKL	1072	G72PKR	1082	G82SKR
1042	E42UKL	1052	E52UKL	1062	E62UKL	1073	G73PKR	1083	G83SKR
1043	E43UKL	1053	E53UKL	1063	E63UKL	1074	G74PKR	1084	G84SKR
1044	E44UKL	1054	E54UKL	1064	E64UKL	1075	G75PKR	1085	G85SKR
1045	E45UKL	1055	E55UKL	1065	E65XKE	1076	G76PKR	1086	G86SKR
1046	E46UKL	1056	E56UKL	1066	F66BKK	1077	G77PKR	1087	G87SKR
1047	E47UKL	1057	E57UKL	1067	F67BKK	1078	G78SKR		
1048	E48UKL	1058	E58UKL	1069	G69PKR	1079	G79SKR		
1049	E49UKL	1059	E59UKL	1070	G70PKR	1080	G80SKR		
1050	E50UKL	1060	E60UKL	1071	G71PKR	1081	G81SKR		

1200	E980NMK	Mercedes-Benz 709D	Reeve Burgess	B20F	1988	Ex Biss, Bishops Stortford, 1990
1201	G201RKK	Mercedes-Benz 709D	Reeve Burgess Beaver	B25F	1989	
1202	G202RKK	Mercedes-Benz 709D	Reeve Burgess Beaver	B25F	1989	
1203	G203RKK	Mercedes-Benz 709D	Reeve Burgess Beaver	B25F	1989	

1204	H204EKO	Mercedes-Benz 709D	Carlyle	B25F	1991	
1401	H395GKO	OBC Omni	OBC	B20F	1991	On extended loan from KCC
1402	F861RYH	Mercedes-Benz 811D	Reeve Burgess Beaver	DP29F	1988	On extended loan from KCC
2159	GGM69W	Leyland Leopard PSU3F/4R	Plaxton Supreme IV Exp	C53F	1981	Ex The Bee Line, 1992
2160	GGM72W	Leyland Leopard PSU3F/4R	Plaxton Supreme IV Exp	C49F	1981	Ex The Bee Line, 1992
2161	LKE648V	Leyland Leopard PSU3E/4RT	Duple Dominant II Exp	C49F	1980	
2162	LKE641V	Leyland Leopard PSU3E/4RT	Duple Dominant II Exp	C49F	1980	
2163	LKE645V	Leyland Leopard PSU3E/4RT	Duple Dominant II Exp	C49F	1980	
2164	YKP975X	Leyland Leopard PSU3E/4R	Duple Dominant II	C53F	1981	Ex New Enterprise, 1990
2166	TSU644	Leyland Tiger TRCTL11/3R	Plaxton Paramount 3200Exp	C53F	1983	Ex New Enterprise, 1994
2167	CKE167Y	Leyland Tiger TRCTL11/3R	Eastern Coach Works B51	C49F	1982	
2168	CKE168Y	Leyland Tiger TRCTL11/3R	Eastern Coach Works B51	C49F	1982	
2169	CKE169Y	Leyland Tiger TRCTL11/3R	Eastern Coach Works B51	C49F	1982	
2170	CKE170Y	Leyland Tiger TRCTL11/3R	Eastern Coach Works B51	C49F	1982	
2171	YSU894	Leyland Tiger TRCTL11/2R	Plaxton Paramount 3200Exp	C53F	1983	Ex Kentish Bus, 1990
2172	YSU895	Leyland Tiger TRCTL11/2R	Plaxton Paramount 3200Exp	C53F	1983	Ex London Buses, 1990
2173	YSU896	Leyland Tiger TRCTL11/2R	Plaxton Paramount 3200Exp	C53F	1983	Ex London Country NE, 1990
2174	YSU897	Leyland Tiger TRCTL11/2R	Plaxton Paramount 3200Exp	C53F	1983	Ex Kentish Bus, 1990
2175	TSU646	Leyland Tiger TRCTL11/3R	Plaxton Paramount 3200Exp	C53F	1983	

2176-2185   Leyland Tiger TRCTL11/3R   Duple Laser Express   C53F*   1983   * 2176-8 are C50F, 2181 is C51F

2176	YLK281	2178	681CXM	2180	YOT607	2182	VAY879	2184	544XVW
2177	445YMU	2179	869SVX	2181	NTK611	2183	TSU636	2185	648WHK

2186	YSU870	Leyland Tiger TRCTL11/3ARH	Plaxton Paramount 3500 3	C53F	1988	
2187	YSU871	Leyland Tiger TRCTL11/3ARH	Plaxton Paramount 3500 3	C53F	1988	
2188	F188HKK	Leyland Tiger TRCTL10/3RZA	Duple 340	C53F	1989	
2189	F189HKK	Leyland Tiger TRCTL10/3RZA	Duple 340	C53F	1989	
2190	ESK987	Leyland Tiger TRCTL11/3R	Duple Caribbean 2	C50F	1985	Ex Brighton & Hove, 1992
2191	ESK988	Leyland Tiger TRCTL11/3R	Duple Caribbean 2	C50F	1985	Ex Brighton & Hove, 1992
2192	YSU872	Leyland Tiger TRCTL11/3RZ	Duple 320	C53F	1989	Ex Park, Hamilton, 1993
2193	YSU873	Leyland Tiger TRCTL11/3RZ	Duple 320	C53F	1989	Ex Park, Hamilton, 1993
2194	J25UNY	Leyland Tiger TRCL10/3ARZM	Plaxton 321	C53F	1992	Ex Bebb, Llantwit Fardre, 1993
2195	J26UNY	Leyland Tiger TRCL10/3ARZM	Plaxton 321	C53F	1992	Ex Bebb, Llantwit Fardre, 1993
2196	J27UNY	Leyland Tiger TRCL10/3ARZM	Plaxton 321	C53F	1992	Ex Bebb, Llantwit Fardre, 1993
2837	VKN837X	Leyland Leopard PSU3F/4R	Willowbrook 003 Mk2	C47F	1982	

3001-3005   Leyland Leopard PSU3D/4R   Alexander AY   B53F   1977-78   Ex Western Scottish, 1993

3001	TSJ64S	3002	TSJ77S	3003	TSJ83S	3004	TSJ86S	3005	TSJ87S

3006	YCS92T	Leyland Leopard PSU3E/4R	Alexander AY	B53F	1978	Ex Western Scottish, 1993
3045	F45ENF	Leyland Lynx LX112L10ZR1R	Leyland	B49F	1988	Ex Shearings, 1991
3046	F46ENF	Leyland Lynx LX112L10ZR1R	Leyland	B49F	1988	Ex Shearings, 1991
3047	F47ENF	Leyland Lynx LX112L10ZR1R	Leyland	B49F	1988	Ex Shearings, 1991
3048	F48ENF	Leyland Lynx LX112L10ZR1R	Leyland	B49F	1988	Ex Shearings, 1991
3456	EKL452K	Leyland Leopard PSU4B/4R	Marshall	B52F	1972	
3462	GKE462L	Leyland Leopard PSU4B/4R	Marshall	B52F	1972	
3463	J463MKL	Dennis Dart 9SDL3012	Plaxton Pointer	B40F	1991	
3464	J464MKL	Dennis Dart 9SDL3012	Plaxton Pointer	B40F	1991	
3465	J465MKL	Dennis Dart 9SDL3012	Plaxton Pointer	B40F	1991	

3466-3471   Dennis Dart 9SDL3017   Plaxton Pointer   B40F   1992

3466	J466OKP	3468	J468OKP	3470	K470SKO	
3467	J467OKP	3469	K469SKO	3471	K471SKO	

3505	NEL128P	Leyland National 11351A/1R	B49F	1976	Ex Wilts & Dorset, 1992
3506	MAR781P	Leyland National 11351/1R	B49F	1976	Ex Wilts & Dorset, 1992
3507	MLJ919P	Leyland National 11351/1R	B49F	1976	Ex Wilts & Dorset, 1992
3521	GKL739N	Leyland National 11351/1R	B49F	1974	
3523	GKL741N	Leyland National 11351/1R	B49F	1974	

3546-3563   Leyland National 11351A/1R   B49F   1976-77

3546	PKP546R	3551	PKP551R	3555	SKR555R	3561	VKE561S
3547	PKP547R	3552	PKP552R	3559	VKE559S	3563	VKE563S
3548	PKP548R	3553	PKP553R	3560	VKE560S	

3601-3610 Volvo B6 Plaxton Pointer B40F 1994

3601 L601EKM	**3603** L603EKM	**3605** L605EKM	**3607** L607EKM	**3609** L609EKM
3602 L602EKM	**3604** L604EKM	**3606** L606EKM	**3608** L608EKM	**3610** L610EKM

3901-3909 Leyland National 11351A/1R DP48F 1977

3901 SKN901R	**3904** SKN904R	**3905** SKN905R	**3908** SKN908R	**3909** SKN909R

4155 CKR155T	Leyland Leopard PSU3E/4RT	Duple Dominant II	C49F	1979	Ex New Enterprise, 1992
5041 JDB108N	Daimler Fleetline CRG6LXB	Northern Counties	H43/32F	1975	Ex London Buslines, 1992
5042 HJA117N	Daimler Fleetline CRG6LXB	Northern Counties	H43/32F	1975	Ex London Buslines, 1992
5105 KKO105P	Bristol VRT/SL3/501	Eastern Coach Works	H43/31F	1975	

5107-5116 Bristol VRT/SL3/6LXB Eastern Coach Works H43/31F 1976

5107 PKM107R	**5109** PKM109R	**5111** PKM111R	**5113** PKM113R	**5116** PKM116R
5108 PKM108R	**5110** PKM110R	**5112** PKM112R	**5114** PKM114R	

5120 PKP120R	Bristol VRT/SL3/501	Eastern Coach Works	H43/31F	1977

5125-5139 Bristol VRT/SL3/6LXB Eastern Coach Works H43/31F 1977-78

5125 WKO125S	**5127** WKO127S	**5132** WKO132S	**5135** WKO135S	**5138** WKO138S
5126 WKO126S	**5128** WKO128S	**5133** WKO133S	**5137** WKO137S	**5139** WKO139S

5201-5210 MCW Metrobus 2 DR102/42 MCW H45/31F 1984

5201 A201OKJ	**5203** A203OKJ	**5205** A205OKJ	**5207** A207OKJ	**5209** A209OKJ
5202 A202OKJ	**5204** A204OKJ	**5206** A206OKJ	**5208** A208OKJ	**5210** A210OKJ

5300 XBF700S	Dennis Dominator DD102	Alexander AL	H43/31F	1978	Ex Potteries, 1983

5302-5306 Dennis Dominator DD129 Willowbrook H43/31F 1980

5302 FKM302V	**5303** FKM303V	**5304** FKM304V	**5305** FKM305V	**5306** FKM306V

5308 XRF23S	Dennis Dominator DD101A	East Lancs	H43/32F	1978	Ex East Staffordshire, 1985
5309 FBF127T	Dennis Dominator DD110A	East Lancs	H43/32F	1979	Ex East Staffordshire, 1985
5313 PRE36W	Dennis Dominator DD120A	East Lancs	H43/32F	1981	Ex East Staffordshire, 1985
5314 PRE38W	Dennis Dominator DD120A	East Lancs	H43/32F	1981	Ex East Staffordshire, 1985
5315 PRE39W	Dennis Dominator DD120A	East Lancs	H43/32F	1981	Ex East Staffordshire, 1985
5317 WWM904W	Dennis Dominator DD120B	Willowbrook	H45/33F	1980	Ex Merseybus, 1986
5318 UBG24V	Dennis Dominator DD120B	Willowbrook	H45/33F	1980	Ex Merseybus, 1986

5441-5445 Leyland Olympian ONTL11/2R Eastern Coach Works CH45/28F 1983 5445 rebodied 1985

5441 GKE441Y	**5442** GKE442Y	**5443** YSU865	**5444** YSU866	**5445** YSU867

5446 WSU475	Leyland Olympian ONTL11/2RSp	Eastern Coach Works	CH45/26F	1985
5447 WSU476	Leyland Olympian ONTL11/2RSp	Eastern Coach Works	CH45/26F	1985
5706 FKM706L	Leyland Atlantean PDR1A/1Sp	MCW	O45/33F	1972
5708 FKM708L	Leyland Atlantean PDR1A/1Sp	MCW	H45/33F	1972

5721-5735 Leyland Atlantean AN68A/1R Northern Counties H43/32F 1976-77 Ex GM Buses, 1987-88

5721 LJA621P	**5724** LJA650P	**5727** SRJ743R	**5730** UNA798S	**5733** LJA652P
5722 LJA626P	**5725** ONF679R	**5728** SRJ746R	**5731** LJA635P	**5734** ONF654R
5723 LJA644P	**5726** ONF680R	**5729** SRJ751R	**5732** LJA648P	**5735** ONF655R

5736 KPJ262W	Leyland Atlantean AN68B/1R	Roe	H43/30F	1981	Ex Luton & District, 1991
5737 KPJ264W	Leyland Atlantean AN68B/1R	Roe	H43/30F	1981	Ex Luton & District, 1991
5738 KPJ280W	Leyland Atlantean AN68B/1R	Roe	H43/30F	1981	Ex Luton & District, 1991
5739 KPJ289W	Leyland Atlantean AN68B/1R	Roe	H43/30F	1981	Ex Luton & District, 1991
5741 XPG161T	Leyland Atlantean AN68A/1R	Park Royal	H43/30F	1978	Ex Luton & District, 1991
5742 XPG164T	Leyland Atlantean AN68A/1R	Park Royal	H43/30F	1978	Ex Luton & District, 1991
5826 URB166S	Bristol VRT/SL3/6LXB	Eastern Coach Works	H43/31F	1977	Ex Bluebird Northern, 1993
5827 WRC833S	Bristol VRT/SL3/501	Eastern Coach Works	H43/31F	1978	Ex Trent, 1993
5828 BRC834T	Bristol VRT/SL3/6LXB	Eastern Coach Works	H43/31F	1979	Ex Trent, 1993
5829 BRC835T	Bristol VRT/SL3/6LXB	Eastern Coach Works	H43/31F	1979	Ex Trent, 1993
5830 BRC837T	Bristol VRT/SL3/6LXB	Eastern Coach Works	H43/31F	1979	Ex Trent, 1993

5831-5886 Bristol VRT/SL3/6LXB Eastern Coach Works H43/31F 1978-80

5831 BKE831T	5842 BKE842T	5855 BKE855T	5869 FKM869V	5881 FKM881V
5832 BKE832T	5843 BKE843T	5856 BKE856T	5873 FKM873V	5882 FKM882V
5833 BKE833T	5845 BKE845T	5857 BKE857T	5874 FKM874V	5883 HKM883V
5835 BKE835T	5846 BKE846T	5863 FKM863V	5875 FKM875V	5884 HKM884V
5837 BKE837T	5847 BKE847T	5864 FKM864V	5876 FKM876V	5885 HKM885V
5838 BKE838T	5848 BKE848T	5865 FKM865V	5877 FKM877V	5886 HKM886V
5839 BKE839T	5852 BKE852T	5866 FKM866V	5878 FKM878V	
5840 BKE840T	5853 BKE853T	5867 FKM867V	5879 FKM879V	
5841 BKE841T	5854 BKE854T	5868 FKM868V	5880 FKM880V	

5888 A888PKR	Leyland Olympian ONLXB/1R	Eastern Coach Works	DPH42/27F	1984
5889 A889PKR	Leyland Olympian ONLXB/1R	Eastern Coach Works	DPH42/27F	1984
5890 A890PKR	Leyland Olympian ONLXB/1R	Eastern Coach Works	DPH42/27F	1984

5891-5900 Leyland Olympian ON6LXB/1RH Northern Counties H45/30F 1988

5891 E891AKN	5893 F893BKK	5895 F895BKK	5897 F897DKK	5899 F899DKK
5892 F892BKK	5894 F894BKK	5896 F896DKK	5898 F898DKK	5900 F900DKK

5901-5905 Leyland Olympian ON2R50G13Z4 Northern Counties H45/30F 1990

5901 G901SKP	5902 G902SKP	5903 G903SKP	5904 G904SKP	5905 G905SKP

5906-5910 Leyland Olympian ON2R50C13Z4 NC Countybus Palatine H47/30F 1993

5906 K906SKR	5907 K907SKR	5908 K908SKR	5909 K909SKR	5910 K910SKR

5911-5925 Volvo Olympian NC Countybus Palatine H47/30F 1994

5911 M911MKM	5913 M913MKM	5915 M915MKM	5917 M917MKM	5919 M919MKM
5912 M912MKM	5914 M914MKM	5916 M916MKM	5918 M918MKM	5920 M920MKM

New Enterprise fleet

4	H301FKL	Mercedes-Benz 811D	Reeve Burgess Beaver	DP25F	1991	
6	F68BKK	Mercedes-Benz 609D	Reeve Burgess	DP19F	1988	Ex Maidstone & District, 1993
7	MPL126W	Leyland Leopard PSU3E/4R	Duple DominantIVExp(1983)	C53F	1981	Ex Barrie, Alexandria, 1988
8	MPL134W	Leyland Leopard PSU3E/4R	Duple DominantIVExp	C53F	1981	Ex Barrie, Alexandria, 1988
12	JKM166V	Leyland Leopard PSU5C/4R	Duple Dominant II	C53F	1980	Ex Maidstone & District, 1988
14	AKP430T	Bedford YMT	Plaxton Supreme III	C53F	1979	Ex Sonner, Gillingham, 1981
15	BNO702T	Bedford YMT	Duple Dominant II Express	C53F	1979	Ex Limebourne, London SW1, 1985
16	CVA110V	Bedford YMT	Plaxton Supreme IV	C45F	1980	Ex Young, Rampton, 1985
18	LSK643	Bedford YNV	Plaxton Paramount 3200 2	C49F	1986	Ex Excelsior, Bournemouth, 1988
23	TSU645	Leyland Tiger TRCTL11/3R	Plaxton Paramount 3200Exp	C53F	1983	Ex Maidstone & District, 1990
24	494WYA	Leyland Tiger TRCTL11/3R	Plaxton Paramount 3500	C57F	1984	Ex PMT, 1990
25	LSK641	Leyland Tiger TRCTL11/3R	Plaxton Paramount 3200	C53F	1983	Ex Mercer, Preston, 1991
26	JUR818V	Bedford YMT	Duple Dominant II	C53F	1979	Ex Ranger, Croydon, 1992
28	642WKR	Bedford YNT	Duple Laser	C53F	1984	Ex Boro'line Maidstone, 1992
29	LPA443W	Bedford YNT	Plaxton Supreme IV	C53F	1980	Ex Cocklin, London SW7, 1993
30	A222DRM	Bedford YNT	Plaxton Paramount 3200	C53F	1984	Ex D J Clarke, Elmswell, 1994
31	G897DEH	Scania K113CRB	Plaxton Paramount 3500 3	C47FT	1990	Ex Happy Days, Woodseaves, 1994
56	FKM266V	MCW Metrobus DR101/10	MCW	H46/30F	1980	Ex Maidstone & District, 1993
57	FKM270V	MCW Metrobus DR104/2	MCW	H46/30F	1980	Ex Maidstone & District, 1993
58	THM658M	Daimler Fleetline CRL6	MCW	H45/32F	1974	Ex Maidstone & District, 1994

Previous registrations

ESK987	B812JPN	VAY879	A182MKE	YSU871	E187XKO	648WHK	A185MKE	LKE645V JKK163V,
ESK988	B815JPN	WSU475	B446WKE	YSU872	G795RNC	642WKR	B202XKM	YSU872
LSK641	KGS494Y	WSU476	B447WKE	YSU873	G796RNC	494WYA	A268MEH,	LKE648V JKK161V,
LSK643	C112AFX	YLK281	A176MKE	YSU894	A107EPA		507EXA,	YSU870
NTK611	A181MKE	YOT607	A180MKE	YSU895	A114EPA		A420HND	YKP975X XGS771X,
TSU636	A183MKE	YSU865	GKE443Y	YSU896	A135EPA	544XVW	A184MKE	YSU873
TSU644	FKL174Y	YSU866	GKE444Y	YSU897	A140EPA	445YMU	A177MKE	F861RYH 164D203
TSU645	FKL173Y	YSU867	GKE445Y	681CXM	A178MKE	LKE641V	JKK162V,	
TSU646	FKL175Y	YSU870	E186XKO	869SVX	A179MKE		YSU871	

Special liveries
1401 (Kent Karrier), 2162/3/70-4/6-83/5/90-6 (Invictaway), 2184 (Olau), 3045-8/469-71/901/4 (Park-and-Ride), 3559, 4155, 5139/210/725/8/31/855/66/7/77/88/93 (Overall advertisements), 5443-7 (Route 101) 5891/8 (Maidstone Initiative)

MARCHWOOD MOTORWAYS

Marchwood Motorways (Southampton) Ltd, 200 Salisbury Road, Totton, Hampshire, SO4 3ZP

Marchwood Motorways was formed in October 1955 by D.H. Osborne and C.I. Arnold to operate contract services in and around the oil refinery at Fawley. For a period, work was also undertaken in South Wales at Haverfordwest and Milford Haven. Various small operators in the Southampton area have been acquired, the most recent being Osgoods of Totton in 1972. Deregulation saw the introduction of the Totton-Link hail-and-ride service which initially used two Iveco minibuses.

The first franchised bus service in the United Kingdom started in 1988 when Solent Blue Line contracted out two routes for which several Leyland Nationals were transferred to the Marchwood fleet. Subsequent new vehicles for Marchwood have often been in Solent Blue Line livery for this operation.

The company gained its present name in 1989. In addition to the pcv fleet there is a large fleet of taxis and self-drive hire vehicles. Vehicles not in Solent Blue Line colours are in a livery of red and cream or white and are housed at Totton.

The franchised Solent Blue Line operation of Marchwood Motorways is demonstrated by their newest vehicle, No.505, an Ikarus Citybus on DAF chassis in Southampton. Without inspection of legal lettering there is nothing to distinguish Marchwood vehicles in this livery from those owned by Solent Blue Line. Alan Simpkins

MARCHWOOD MOTORWAYS

213	H711LOL	Dennis Dart 9SDL3002	Carlyle Dartline	B36F	1990	
214	H712LOL	Dennis Dart 9.8SDL3004	Carlyle Dartline	B40F	1991	
288	D647ETR	Iveco Daily 49.10	Robin Hood City Nippy	B21F	1987	
289	D648ETR	Iveco Daily 49.10	Robin Hood City Nippy	B21F	1987	
290	F730OOT	Iveco Daily 49.10	Robin Hood City Nippy	B23F	1988	
291	F731OOT	Iveco Daily 49.10	Robin Hood City Nippy	B23F	1988	
292	H975EOR	Iveco Daily 49.10	Phoenix	B23F	1991	
293	G364FOP	Iveco Daily 49.10	Carlyle Dailybus II	B25F	1990	Ex Strathclyde, 1991
408	PJT262R	Leyland National 11351A/1R		B49F	1976	Ex Solent Blue Line, 1988
409	PJT264R	Leyland National 11351A/1R		B49F	1976	Ex Solent Blue Line, 1988
413	PJT271R	Leyland National 11351A/1R		B49F	1976	Ex Solent Blue Line, 1988
416	UFX850S	Leyland National 11351A/1R		B49F	1977	Ex Solent Blue Line, 1988
502	F246RJX	DAF SB220LC550	Optare Delta	B47F	1989	
503	J45GCX	DAF SB220LC550	Optare Delta	B49F	1992	
504	L509EHD	DAF SB220LC550	Ikarus Citibus	B48F	1993	
505	L510EHD	DAF SB220LC550	Ikarus Citibus	B48F	1993	
	VTA989S	Bedford YMT	Plaxton Supreme III	C53F	1977	Ex Yendell, Witheridge, 1986
	CEL105T	Bedford YMT	Plaxton Supreme III	C53F	1979	Ex Day, North Common, 1986
	VFB617T	Bedford YMT	Caetano Alpha	C53F	1979	Ex Fryer, Bristol, 1986
	BHO442V	Leyland Leopard PSU5C/4R	Duple Dominant II	C55F	1980	
	UFX630X	Leyland Tiger TRCTL11/3R	Duple	C53F	1981	
	225ASV	Bova EL26-581	Bova Europa	C52F	1982	Ex Dodsworth, Scarborough, 1989
	C82NNV	DAF SB3000DKSB585	Caetano Algarve	C53F	1986	
	C83NNV	DAF SB2300DHS585	Caetano Algarve	C53F	1986	
	C337VRY	Bova FLD12-250	Bova Futura	C57F	1986	
	D131CJF	Bova FHD12-290	Bova Futura	C49FT	1987	
	D258JPR	Ford Transit 190	Deansgate	B12F	1987	
	D259JPR	Ford Transit 190	Deansgate	B12F	1987	
	F629SRP	LAG Panoramic	LAG	C49FT	1989	
	F630SRP	LAG Panoramic	LAG	C49FT	1989	
	F764XNH	LAG Panoramic	LAG	C49FT	1989	
	F247RJX	DAF SB2305DHTD585	Duple 340	C57F	1989	
	F248RJX	DAF SB2305DHTD585	Duple 340	C57F	1989	
	F851YJX	DAF SB2305DHTD585	Plaxton Paramount 3500 2	C53F	1989	
	G722VTR	DAF Sherpa 400	DAF	B16F	1989	
	G504WOR	DAF Sherpa 200	DAF	B12F	1990	
	H391CJF	MAN 10-180	Caetano Algarve	C35F	1990	
	H51VNH	Volvo B10M-60	Jonckheere Deauville P599	C51FT	1990	
	H186EJF	Toyota HDB30R	Caetano Optimo	C21F	1991	
	H187EJF	Toyota HDB30R	Caetano Optimo	C18F	1991	
	H712KPR	Ford Transit	Bristol Street	B14F	1991	
	J851KHD	DAF SB2305DHTD585	Van Hool Alizée	C49FT	1992	
	J852KHD	DAF SB2305DHTD585	Van Hool Alizée	C49FT	1992	
	J853KHD	DAF SB2305DHTD585	Van Hool Alizée	C49FT	1992	
	J854KHD	DAF SB2305DHS585	Plaxton Paramount 3500 3	C55F	1992	
	K430TLJ	Ford Transit	Ford	B12F	1992	
	K232WNH	MAN 16-290	Jonckheere Deauville P599	C51FT	1993	
	K233WNH	MAN 16-290	Jonckheere Deauville P599	C51FT	1993	
	K234WNH	MAN 16-290	Jonckheere Deauville P599	C51FT	1993	

Previous registration
225ASV   SMY621X

Named vehicle
L510EHD County of Hampshire

MERCURY PASSENGER SERVICES

S.L. Edgecombe, Units 1-7 Gamma Road, Kingsnorth Industrial Estate, Hoo, Kent

Mercury Passenger Services has gained a number of Kent County Council contracts in the Maidstone and Medway areas since the end of March 1991, consolidating these with some commercial operations. Services extend along the Hoo peninsula to the north and as far south as Goudhurst in the Kentish hop country. In January 1993 a Kent Karrier network was gained in the Medway Towns area.

Vehicles have generally operated in as-acquired liveries, but a maroon livery was introduced in 1992 for the former London Buses Optare-bodied City Pacers.

Whilst Mercury has generally operated with acquired vehicles, freshness was brought to the fleet in the form of two new Omnis provided by Kent County Council for Kent Karrier services which started in January 1993. K726SKP, photographed in Military Road, Chatham on 19th August 1993, was however working on a commercial route rather than its usual operation. John Grubb

MERCURY PASSENGER SERVICES

1005	JJG5P	Leyland Atlantean AN68/1R	Eastern Coach Works	H43/31F	1976	Ex Eastbourne Buses, 1992
1338	D338JUM	Volkswagen LT55	Optare CityPacer	B25F	1986	Ex London Buses, 1991
1342	PJJ342S	Leyland National 10351A/1R		B41F	1977	Ex East Kent, 1991
1361	D361JUM	Volkswagen LT55	Optare CityPacer	DP25F	1986	Ex London Buses, 1991
1609	D609NOE	MCW Metrorider MF150/3	MCW	B23F	1987	On extended hire from West Midlands Travel
1813	D813KWT	Freight Rover Sherpa 374D	Dormobile	DP16F	1987	Ex West Riding, 1991
1888	JJG888P	Leyland National 11351/1R		B49F	1976	Ex East Kent, 1991
	DOC33V	Leyland National 2 NL116L11/1R	B37D		1980	On extended hire from West Midlands Travel
	JHE190W	MCW Metrobus DR104/6	MCW	H46/31F	1981	Ex Stevenson, Uttoxeter, 1992
	HIL4521	Mercedes-Benz L207D	Whittaker	C12F	1982	Ex Frith, Southport, 1991
	438UHT	Auwaerter Neoplan N122/3	Auwaerter Skyliner	CH53/18CT	1982	Ex Evans, Chew Stoke, 1992
	C53HDT	Dennis Domino SDA1202	Optare	B33F	1985	Ex South Yorkshire, 1993
	K645SKK	OCC Omni	OCC	B20F	1992	
	K726SKP	OCC Omni	OCC	DP19F	1992	

Previous registrations

HIL4521	JTU837Y
438UHT	WFH931X, HHF15

NU-VENTURE ⟳

Nu-Venture Coaches Ltd, 86 Mill Hall, Aylesford, Maidstone, Kent, ME20 7JN

The long-established local coaching firm of Nu-Venture has operated a number of contracts for Kent County Council since deregulation, and has supplemented these by commercial operations to the west of Maidstone, sometimes taking advantage of what would otherwise be light running between contract work and the home base.

As well as a number of services into rural areas, Nu-Venture have a Monday to Friday contract from Kent County Council for a local service in Maidstone via Queens Road to Banky Meadow. AYR345T, in the High Street on 9th September 1993, derived from the Boro'line Maidstone fleet when that was dispersed in 1992, and was originally owned by London Buses. John Grubb

NU-VENTURE

PTT106R	Bristol LH6L	Plaxton Supreme III Exp	C43F	1977	Ex Worthington, Collingham, 1989
AYR345T	Leyland National 10351A/2R		B36D	1979	Ex Boro'line Maidstone, 1992
3558RU	Leyland Tiger TRCTL11/3R	Duple Laser	C51F	1983	Ex Warren, Neath, 1991
8421RU	Leyland Tiger TRCTL11/2R	Duple Laser	C53F	1984	Ex Shearings, Wigan, 1991
E134NDE	Talbot Pullman	Talbot	B22F	1988	Ex Tenby Bus & Coach, Tenby, 1990
NIW4121	DAF SB2305DHS585	Caetano Algarve	C49FT	1988	Ex D Coaches, Morriston, 1992
NIW4120	Dennis Javelin 12SDA1907	Caetago Algarve	C51FT	1990	
G75TKN	Talbot Pullman	Talbot	DP22F	1990	
H192EKM	Talbot Pullman	Talbot	B22F	1991	
L866BEA	Iveco Daily 59.12	Marshall	B29F	1993	

Previous registrations

NIW4120	G92SKR
NIW4121	E740JAY
3558RU	HBH427Y, 9GUV, SWN753Y
8421RU	A157MNE

OXFORD BUS COMPANY

City of Oxford Motor Services Ltd, Cowley Road, Oxford, OX4 2DJ

The Oxford Bus Company, as it is now marketed, was sold by the NBC to a management-led team on 15th January 1987. The High Wycombe operations of Berks Bucks were absorbed in November 1990 and are now operated as a separate unit; Wycombe Bus has the first Leyland-Nationals to be owned by the company. Ownership passed to the Go-Ahead Group on 1st March 1994.

Operations are largely confined to the areas around Oxford and High Wycombe, other routes having been transferred to the offshoot South Midland company which in turn was taken over by Thames Transit in December 1988. There is a frequent City Link service along the M40 to London, together with a similar facility direct to Heathrow and Gatwick Airports. Another interesting operation is the Park-and-Ride service between outlying car parks and the city centre.

Oxford has caused some interest by purchasing 26 redundant Leyland Titans from London Buses Ltd. These are ousting the older examples of the Bristol VRT type. Four electric Optare Metroriders have also been taken into stock.

The standard livery is red with white roof and black skirt, replacing an earlier scheme of poppy red with white relief. City Link vehicles carry dark blue, deep yellow and white, applied in NBC-derived style. The fleet is garaged at the main address and in High Wycombe.

One of 26 Leyland Titans purchased from London Buses, No.960 is seen leaving Blackbird Leys Estate. These vehicles are also used on the Barton Estate routes. Gerald Mead

Left **Oxford caused something of a surprise by ordering new Willowbrook bodies for seven Leyland Leopards cascaded from London service in 1990/1. No.613 represents the type.**
Malcolm McDonald

Centre **The acquisition of the High Wycombe operations of Berks Bucks finally brought Leyland Nationals into the fleet in 1990 after Oxford had managed to eschew the type since its launch.**
Malcolm McDonald

Below left **A surprising development was the arrival of four Optare Metroriders in 1993 specially modified to run as rechargeable electric vehicles. No.801 is the first of the batch.**
Malcolm McDonald

Below right **More conventional were fifteen orthodox Optare Metroriders delivered in 1990 as part of an upgrading of the minibus fleet. No.771 demonstrates the Oxford City Nipper livery in this view in the town centre.**
Malcolm King

Vehicles numbered above 1000 are allocated to the Wycombe Bus fleet

50-55
Dennis Javelin 12SDA2118 — Plaxton Première 320 — C53F — 1992

50	K750UJO	52	K752UJO	54	K754UJO
51	K751UJO	53	K753UJO	55	K755UJO

100	YPJ209Y	Leyland Tiger TRCTL11/3R	Plaxton Paramount 3200	C50F	1983	Ex The Bee Line, 1990
105	EBW105Y	Leyland Tiger TRCTL11/3R	Duple Dominant IV Express	C50F	1983
107	EBW107Y	Leyland Tiger TRCTL11/3R	Duple Dominant IV Express	C50F	1983
108	EBW108Y	Leyland Tiger TRCTL11/3R	Duple Dominant IV Express	C50F	1983
111	A111MUD	Leyland Tiger TRCTL11/3RH	Plaxton Paramount 3200ExpC51F	1984
112	A112MUD	Leyland Tiger TRCTL11/3RH	Plaxton Paramount 3200ExpC51F	1984
113	A113MUD	Leyland Tiger TRCTL11/3RH	Plaxton Paramount 3200ExpC51F	1984
114	A114MUD	Leyland Tiger TRCTL11/3RH	Plaxton Paramount 3200ExpC51F	1984

115-119
Leyland Tiger TRCTL11/3RH — Plaxton Paramount 3200ExpC50F — 1984

115	A115PBW	117	A117PBW	119	A119PBW
116	A116PBW	118	A118PBW		

120-124
Leyland Tiger TRCTL11/3RH — Plaxton Paramount 3200 2 — C51F — 1984

120	B120UUD	121	B121UUD	122	B122UUD	123	B123UUD	124	B124UUD

130-134
DAF MB230LT615 — Plaxton Paramount 3500 3 — C53F — 1988

130	E130YUD	131	E131YUD	132	E132YUD	133	E133YUD	134	E134YUD

135-139
DAF SB3000DKV601 — Plaxton Paramount 3500 3 — C53F — 1989

135	F135LJO	136	F136LJO	137	F137LJO	138	F138LJO	139	F139LJO

140	J140NJO	DAF SB2305DHS585	Plaxton Paramount 3200 3	C53F	1991
141	J141NJO	DAF SB2305DHS585	Plaxton Paramount 3200 3	C53F	1991

150-155
Volvo B10M-62 — Plaxton Première 350 — C53F — 1993

150	L150HUD	152	L152HUD	154	L154HUD
151	L151HUD	153	L153HUD	155	L155HUD

201-224
Leyland Olympian ONLXB/1R — Eastern Coach Works — H45/28D — 1982-83

201	VJO201X	206	VJO206X	211	WWL211X	216	BBW216Y	221	CUD221Y
202	VJO202X	207	WWL207X	212	WWL212X	217	BBW217Y	222	CUD222Y
203	VJO203X	208	WWL208X	213	BBW213Y	218	BBW218Y	223	CUD223Y
204	VJO204X	209	WWL209X	214	BBW214Y	219	CUD219Y	224	CUD224Y
205	VJO205X	210	WWL210X	215	BBW215Y	220	CUD220Y		

225-229
Leland Olympian ONLXB/1RH — Alexander RL — H47/26D — 1988

225	E225CFC	226	E226CFC	227	E227CFC	228	E228CFC	229	E229CFC

230-235
Leyland Olympian ON2R50G16Z4 — Alexander RL — H47/26D — 1990

230	G230VWL	232	G232VWL	234	G234VWL
231	G231VWL	233	G233VWL	235	G235VWL

236	FWL778Y	Leyland Olympian ONLXB/1R	Eastern Coach Works	H45/32F	1983	Ex UKAEA, Harwell, 1991
237	FWL779Y	Leyland Olympian ONLXB/1R	Eastern Coach Works	H45/32F	1983	Ex UKAEA, Harwell, 1991
238	FWL780Y	Leyland Olympian ONLXB/1R	Eastern Coach Works	H45/32F	1983	Ex UKAEA, Harwell, 1991
239	FWL781Y	Leyland Olympian ONLXB/1R	Eastern Coach Works	H45/32F	1983	Ex UKAEA, Harwell, 1991

476-512
Bristol VRT/SL3/6LXB — Eastern Coach Works — H43/27D — 1978-81

476	HUD476S	481	HUD481S	494	HUD494W	500	HUD500W	507	KJO507W
477	HUD477S	486	OUD486T	499	HUD499W	505	KJO505W	512	PFC512W

611	RFC11T	Leyland Leopard PSU3E/4R	Willowbrook Warrior(1991)	B48F	1978	
612	WPD27Y	Leyland Leopard PSU3G/4R	Willowbrook Warrior(1991)	B48F	1982	Ex The Bee Line, 1990
613	RFC13T	Leyland Leopard PSU3E/4R	Willowbrook Warrior(1991)	B48F	1978	
614	RFC14T	Leyland Leopard PSU3E/4R	Willowbrook Warrior(1991)	B48F	1978	
627	MUD27W	Leyland Leopard PSU3F/4R	Willowbrook Warrior(1990)	B48F	1981	
631	VUD31X	Leyland Leopard PSU3G/4R	Willowbrook Warrior(1991)	B48F	1982	
633	VUD33X	Leyland Leopard PSU3G/4R	Willowbrook Warrior(1990)	B48F	1982	
750	D750SJO	MCW Metrorider MF150/13	MCW	B25F	1987	

751-757 — MCW Metrorider MF150/26 — MCW — B25F — 1987

751	E751VJO	753	E753VJO	755	E755VJO	757	E757VJO
752	E752VJO	754	E754VJO	756	E756VJO		

No.	Reg	Model	Body	Type	Year	Notes
758	E758XWL	MCW Metrorider MF150/51	MCW	B25F	1987	
759	E759XWL	MCW Metrorider MF150/51	MCW	B25F	1987	
761	E761XWL	MCW Metrorider MF150/51	MCW	B25F	1987	
762	E762XWL	MCW Metrorider MF150/51	MCW	B25F	1987	
763	F763LBW	MCW Metrorider MF150/114	MCW	B25F	1989	
764	F501ANY	MCW Metrorider MF150/109	MCW	B23F	1989	Ex Merthyr Tydfil, 1989
765	F502ANY	MCW Metrorider MF150/109	MCW	B23F	1989	Ex Merthyr Tydfil, 1989
766	F503ANY	MCW Metrorider MF150/109	MCW	B23F	1989	Ex Merthyr Tydfil, 1989
767	F504ANY	MCW Metrorider MF150/109	MCW	B23F	1989	Ex Merthyr Tydfil, 1989
768	F505CBO	MCW Metrorider MF150/105	MCW	B25F	1989	Ex Merthyr Tydfil, 1989

769-783 — Optare Metrorider — Optare — B28F — 1990

769	G769WFC	772	G772WFC	775	G775WFC	778	G778WFC	781	G781WFC
770	G770WFC	773	G773WFC	776	G776WFC	779	G779WFC	782	G782WFC
771	G771WFC	774	G774WFC	777	G777WFC	780	G780WFC	783	G783WFC

No.	Reg	Model	Body	Type	Year
801	L801HJO	Optare Metrorider(electric)	Optare	B18F	1993
802	L802HJO	Optare Metrorider(electric)	Optare	B18F	1993
803	L803HJO	Optare Metrorider(electric)	Optare	B18F	1993
804	L804HJO	Optare Metrorider(electric)	Optare	B18F	1993

950-975 — Leyland Titan TNLXB2RR — Leyland — H44/26D* — 1981-83 Ex London Buses, 1993/4

950	GYE280W	956	KYV519X	962	KYV530X	968	NUW661Y	974	NUW635Y
951	KYV516X	957	KYN291X	963	OHV727Y	969	KYV510X	975	A869SUL
952	KYN300X	958	KYV370X	964	OHV745Y	970	KYN308X		
953	KYV317X	959	NUW667Y	965	OHV783Y	971	KYV457X		
954	KYV328X	960	OHV711Y	966	KYV381X	972			
955	KYV452X	961	KYV524X	967	KYV392X	973	KYV493X		

No.	Reg	Model	Body	Type	Year	Notes
999	PWL999W	Leyland Olympian B45/TL11/2R	Alexander RL	H50/34D	1980	Ex Singapore Bus (Leyland demonstrator), 1987
1104	EBW104Y	Leyland Tiger TRCTL11/3R	Duple Dominant IV Express	C51F	1983	
1106	EBW106Y	Leyland Tiger TRCTL11/3R	Duple Dominant IV Express	C51F	1983	
1109	EBW109Y	Leyland Tiger TRCTL11/3R	Duple Dominant IV Express	C50F	1983	
1110	EBW110Y	Leyland Tiger TRCTL11/3R	Duple Dominant IV Express	C50F	1983	

1321-1353 — Leyland National 11351/1R — B49F — 1974-75 Ex The Bee Line, 1990

1321	TBL165M	1344	KPA357P	1351	KPA377P
1328	TBL172M	1346	KPA359P	1353	KPA384P

No.	Reg	Model	Type	Year	Notes
1354	KPA390P	Leyland National 11351A/1R	B45F	1976	Ex The Bee Line, 1990
1356	NPJ481R	Leyland National 11351A/1R	B49F	1976	Ex The Bee Line, 1990
1360	TPE158S	Leyland National 11351A/1R	B49F	1978	Ex The Bee Line, 1990
1377	THX177S	Leyland National 10351A/2R	DP41F	1978	Ex London Buses, 1993
1384	VPF296S	Leyland National 11351A/1R	B49F	1978	Ex The Bee Line, 1990

1401-1405 — Leyland Lynx LX112L10ZR1S — Leyland — B49F — 1988 Ex The Bee Line, 1990

1401	F556NJM	1402	F557NJM	1403	F558NJM	1404	F559NJM	1405	F560NJM

No.	Reg	Model	Body	Type	Year	Notes
1508	MRJ8W	Bristol VRT/SL3/6LXB	Eastern Coach Works	DPH41/29F	1980	Ex Mayne, Manchester, 1991
1509	MRJ9W	Bristol VRT/SL3/6LXB	Eastern Coach Works	DPH41/29F	1980	Ex Mayne, Manchester, 1991

1543-1555 — Bristol VRT/SL3/6LXB — Eastern Coach Works — H43/31F — 1976 Ex The Bee Line, 1990

1543	GGM110W	1546	HJB453W	1549	HJB456W	1552	HJB459W
1544	HJB451W	1547	HJB454W	1550	HJB457W	1554	HJB461W
1545	HJB452W	1548	HJB455W	1551	HJB458W	1555	HJB462W

No.	Reg	Model	Body	Type	Year	Notes
1563	CJH124V	Bristol VRT/SL3/6LXB	Eastern Coach Works	DPH41/25F	1980	Ex The Bee Line, 1990
1760	E760XWL	MCW Metrorider MF150/51	MCW	B25F	1987	
1822	D922UTF	Leyland Olympian ONLXB/1RH	Eastern Coach Works	CH39/21F	1986	Ex The Bee Line, 1990
1823	D923UTF	Leyland Olympian ONLXB/1RH	Eastern Coach Works	CH39/21F	1986	Ex The Bee Line, 1990
1824	D924UTF	Leyland Olympian ONLXB/1RH	Eastern Coach Works	CH39/21F	1986	Ex The Bee Line, 1990

Special liveries
Park and Ride : 225-8, 954/8/99
Overall advertisements : 229/34, 627/33, 971, 1351

PEOPLE'S PROVINCIAL

Provincial Bus Co. Ltd, Gosport Road, Hoeford, Fareham, Hampshire, PO16 0ST

People's Provincial is the fleetname of the Provincial Bus Company, which was the successor to the Provincial Tramways Company Ltd. This started horse tramways in Portsmouth in 1873, and a subsidiary operation followed in Gosport in 1884. The Portsmouth operation passed to Portsmouth Corporation Tramways Department, but the Gosport tramway continued until electrification in 1905. Motor-buses were introduced in 1910 and the tramway was eventually replaced in 1929 when the title of the company was changed to Gosport & Fareham Omnibus Company, when the Provincial fleetname was introduced. The company became part of the National Bus Company in 1970, and was augmented by the addition of the Fareham depots and operations of Hants & Dorset in 1983.

With the sale by the government of the NBC subsidiaries, Provincial became an employee co-ownership scheme, the only NBC fleet to have been sold in this way.

In 1988 day-time operations were extended into Portsmouth, and since then Hampshire County Council contracts have been secured. Notable among these are services formerly worked by Blue Admiral to the north of the city.

The livery is in two shades of green with cream. The depot is on the site of the original tram depot at Hoeford.

Much of People's Provincial fleet is composed of second-hand Leyland Nationals from a wide range of sources. No.392 is one of a batch acquired from Southdown in 1988, having been amongst the first of the type delivered to that fleet in 1973, and was tracked down in Petersfield.
Alan Simpkins

Several second-hand Bristol VRTs have been drawn into the fleet in recent times. No.217 is a dual-door example acquired from Bristol in 1994.
David Harman

All of the minibuses in the fleet are Ivecos, bodied by four different manufacturers. No.139 is the last of twelve delivered in 1992 with Phoenix bodywork.
Malcolm King

The following batch of seven Ivecos was bodied by the revived Marshall concern. No.144 is an example.
Alan Simpkins

The oldest minibuses in the fleet are seven which survive from the 1986 order bodied by Robin Hood. The driver of No.121 checks some details. Malcolm King

PEOPLE'S PROVINCIAL

1	A301KJT	Leyland National 2 NL116L11/1R		DP47F	1984
2	A302KJT	Leyland National 2 NL116L11/1R		DP47F	1984

13-22 — Leyland National 1151/2R/0403 — B44D — 1972-73

13	HOR413L	15	HOR415L	17	HOR417L	19	PCG919M	21	PCG921M
14	HOR414L	16	HOR416L	18	PCG918M	20	PCG920M	22	PCG922

23	RUF37R	Leyland National 11351A/2R		B49F	1977	Ex Rennie, Dunfermline, 1988

24-33 — Leyland National 11351/2R — B44F — 1974-75

24	UAA224M	27	GCR727N	29	JBP129P	31	JBP131P	33	JBP133P
26	UAA226M	28	GCR728N	30	JBP130P	32	JBP132P		

34-44 — Leyland National 11351A/2R — B44D — 1976-79

34	LTP634P	37	MOW637R	40	SBK740S	43	UPO443T
35	LTP635P	38	PTR238S	41	TPX41T	44	UPO444T
36	MOW636R	39	PTR239S	42	TPX42T		

51	NPD130L	Leyland National 1151/1R/0402		B49F	1973	Ex London Country, 1983
52	NPD131L	Leyland National 1151/1R/0402		B49F	1973	Ex London Country, 1983
53	NPD132L	Leyland National 1151/1R/0402		B49F	1973	Ex London Country, 1983
59	HTG470N	Leyland National 11351/1R		B52F	1975	Ex National Welsh, 1987
63	MJT880P	Leyland National 11351/1R		B49F	1976	Ex Hants & Dorset, 1983
64	KDW338P	Leyland National 11351/1R		B49F	1976	Ex National Welsh, 1987

65-72 — Leyland National 11351A/1R — B49F — 1977-78 Ex Hants & Dorset, 1983

65	RJT147R	67	SPR39R	70	UFX847S	72	VFX980S
66	RJT148R	68	SPR40R	71	UFX848S		

73	EEL893V	Leyland National 11351A/1R		DP52F	1979	Ex Hants & Dorset, 1983
74	GLJ674N	Leyland National 11351/1R		B48F	1974	Ex Hants & Dorset, 1983
75	WFX257S	Leyland National 11351A/1R		DP48F	1978	Ex Hants & Dorset, 1983
77	KDW340P	Leyland National 11351/1R		B49F	1975	Ex National Welsh, 1987
100	BDL65T	Bedford YMT	Plaxton Supreme IV	C53F	1979	Ex Solent Blue Line, 1993

118-127   Iveco Daily 49.10   Robin Hood City Nippy   B19F*   1986   * 127 is B21F

118	D118DRV	120	D120DRV	122	D122DRV	127	D127DRV
119	D119DRV	121	D121DRV	123	D123DRV		

128-139   Iveco Daily 49.10   Phoenix   B24F   1992

128	F128SBP	131	F131SBP	134	F134TCR	137	G137WOW
129	F129SBP	132	F132SBP	135	F135TCR	138	G138WOW
130	F130SBP	133	F133TCR	136	F136TCR	139	G139WOW

140-146   Iveco Daily 49.10   Marshall   B23F   1992

140	J140KPX	142	J142KPX	144	J144KPX	146	J146KPX
141	J141KPX	143	J143KPX	145	J145KPX		

160-165   Iveco Daily 59.12   Wadham Stringer   B27F   1993

160	K160PPO	162	K162PPO	164	K164PPO		
161	K161PPO	163	K163PPO	165	K165PPO		

No.	Reg.	Type	Body	Config	Year	History
166	L166TRV	Iveco Daily 59.12	Marshall	B27F	1993	
203	WTN658H	Leyland Atlantean PDR2/1R	Alexander J	H48/35F	1970	Ex Waddon, Bedwas, 1988
208	AUP715S	Bristol VRT/SL3/6LXB	Eastern Coach Works	H43/31F	1977	Ex Northumbria, 1989
209	SFJ101R	Bristol VRT/SL3/6LXB	Eastern Coach Works	H43/31F	1977	Ex Western National, 1993
210	UTO836S	Bristol VRT/SL3/501	Eastern Coach Works	H43/31F	1977	Ex Western National, 1993
211	AFJ748T	Bristol VRT/SL3/6LXB	Eastern Coach Works	H43/31F	1979	Ex Western National, 1993
212	AFJ752T	Bristol VRT/SL3/6LXB	Eastern Coach Works	H43/31F	1979	Ex Western National, 1993
213	AFJ763T	Bristol VRT/SL3/6LXB	Eastern Coach Works	H43/31F	1979	Ex Western National, 1993
214	MOD571P	Bristol VRT/SL3/6LXB	Eastern Coach Works	H43/31F	1979	Ex Western National, 1993
215	NTC573R	Bristol VRT/SL3/6LXB	Eastern Coach Works	H43/27D	1977	Ex Bristol, 1994
216	RHT503S	Bristol VRT/SL3/6LXB	Eastern Coach Works	H43/27D	1978	Ex Bristol, 1994
217	RHT504S	Bristol VRT/SL3/6LXB	Eastern Coach Works	H43/27D	1978	Ex Bristol, 1994
218	RHT512S	Bristol VRT/SL3/6LXB	Eastern Coach Works	H43/27D	1978	Ex Bristol, 1994
219	TWS908T	Bristol VRT/SL3/6LXB	Eastern Coach Works	H43/27D	1979	Ex Bristol, 1994
303	NFN79M	Leyland National 1151/1R/2402		B49F	1974	Ex National Welsh, 1987
305	NPD146L	Leyland National 1151/1R/0402		B49F	1973	Ex London Country, 1983
306	NPD154L	Leyland National 1151/1R/0402		B49F	1973	Ex London Country, 1983
350	NPD128L	Leyland National 1151/1R/0402		B49F	1973	Ex London Country, 1983
355	GHB684N	Leyland National 11351/1R		B52F	1974	Ex National Welsh, 1987
361	KDW334P	Leyland National 11351/1R		B49F	1974	Ex National Welsh, 1987
369	SPR41R	Leyland National 11351A/1R		B49F	1977	Ex Hants & Dorset, 1983
375	WFX253S	Leyland National 11351A/1R		DP48F	1978	Ex Hants & Dorset, 1983
378	KDW343P	Leyland National 11351/1R		B49F	1976	Ex National Welsh, 1987
379	NWO480R	Leyland National 11351A/1R		B49F	1976	Ex National Welsh, 1987
381	NPD135L	Leyland National 1151/1R/0402		B49F	1973	Ex London Country, 1983
382	PHA491M	Leyland National 11351/1R		B49F	1974	Ex Midland Red East, 1983
383	NOE561R	Leyland National 11351A/1R		B49F	1976	Ex Midland Red East, 1983
384	PUK642R	Leyland National 11351A/1R		B49F	1977	Ex Midland Red East, 1983
385	NPD134L	Leyland National 1151/1R/0402		B49F	1973	Ex London Country, 1983
386	NWO490R	Leyland National 11351A/1R		B49F	1976	Ex National Welsh, 1987
388	PKG735R	Leyland National 11351A/1R		B49F	1977	Ex National Welsh, 1987
389	SKG919S	Leyland National 11351A/1R		B49F	1977	Ex National Welsh, 1987

390-394   Leyland National 1151/1R/0102   B49F   1973   Ex Southdown, 1988

390	BCD817L	391	BCD818L	392	BCD819L	393	BCD821L	394	BCD824L

396	HTX726N	Leyland National 11351/1R		B51F	1975	Ex Rennie, Dunfermline, 1988

401-414   Leyland National 10351A/2R   B36D   1976-79 Ex London Buses, 1991

401	KJD528P	404	AYR331T	407	THX234S	410	THX115S	413	AYR341T
402	THX248S	405	AYR334T	408	BYW415V	411	THX131S	414	YYE276T
403	AYR299T	406	YYE278T	409	KJD511P	412	THX242S		

591	NFX130P	Daimler Fleetline CRL6-30	Alexander AD	CO43/31F	1976	Ex Bournemouth, 1991
592	NFX131P	Daimler Fleetline CRL6-30	Alexander AD	CO43/31F	1976	Ex Bournemouth, 1991

Special liveries
Overall advertisements : 65/8, 71/2, 303/83/8/94, 405/13

POYNTER'S

R.J. & B.J. Poynter, Sunray, Churchfield Way, Wye, Ashford, Kent, TN25 5EQ

Poynter's have developed a stake in Kent County Council contract work on rural routes in the Ashford and Canterbury areas since deregulation. Although there was something of a setback when routes were lost in the 1992 tendering round at Ashford, there have been subsequent gains in the Canterbury area and from the withdrawal of Westbus from their Ashford base in the autumn of 1993. There is also a strong presence on local works and schools contracts.

The fleet carries a livery of cream with yellow and orange.

POYNTER'S

Reg	Type	Body	Seating	Year	History
NFM831M	Leyland National 1151/1R/0405		DP49F	1973	Ex Seabrook Coach, Hythe, 1991
GVV887N	Leyland National 11351/1R		B49F	1975	Ex PMT, 1993
KRE279P	Leyland National 11351/1R		B52F	1975	Ex PMT, 1993
KDW339P	Leyland National 11351/1R		B49F	1975	Ex Westbus, Ashford, 1993
YBM938S	DAF MB200DKL600	Plaxton Supreme III	C57F	1978	Ex Wells, Brixham, 1990
XWG639T	Leyland Atlantean AN68A/1R	Roe	H45/29D	1978	Ex TML, Folkestone, 1994
XWG647T	Leyland Atlantean AN68A/1R	Roe	H45/29D	1978	Ex Linkfast, Hadleigh, 1994
HMA562T	Leyland National 10351B/1R		B44F	1978	Ex Crosville Wales, 1991
GMB665T	Leyland National 10351B/1R		B44F	1978	Ex Crosville Wales, 1991
MCA674T	Leyland National 10351B/1R		B44F	1979	Ex PMT, 1993
LLL173V	Ford Transit 190	Robin Hood	C16F	1980	Ex Capital, West Drayton, 1986
RJI2717	DAF MB200DKTL600	Van Hool Alizée	C49DT	1982	Ex Haslam, London N8, 1993
8465LJ	DAF SB2300DHS585	Berkhof Esprite 350	C49FT	1983	Ex Travelfar, Henfield, 1991
6769FM	DAF SB2300DHS585	Berkhof Esprite 340	C49FT	1984	Ex UMBH, Southend, 1990
A409JPB	Kässbohrer Setra S228DT	Kässbohrer Tornado	CH54/20CT	1984	Ex Warren, Alton, 1994
2448UE	DAF SB2300DHS585	Berkhof Esprite 340	C57F	1985	Ex Travelfar, Henfield, 1991
3318VU	DAF SB2300DHS585	LAG Galaxy	C53F	1985	Ex D Coaches, Morriston, 1992
C424AHT	Ford Transit 190	Carlyle	B16F	1986	Ex Pickford, Grittleton, 1991

Previous registrations

A409JPB	A848UGB, WLO471
RJI2717	XJS971X, 279AUF, 318DHR, HAS914X
6769FM	A166OHJ
8465LJ	LHK645Y
2448UE	B688BTW
3318VU	C770FEP

Named vehicles

RJI2717 Princess Anne, 8465LJ Princess Caroline

An increasing level of success in Kent County Council tendering has resulted in Poynters developing a fleet of six Leyland Nationals. GMB665T hailed from Crosville Wales in 1991, and was photographed in Faversham working a service across the Seasalter flats to Whitstable.
Alan Simpkins

RAMBLER

Mrs M. & C. Rowland and J. Goodwin, West Ridge Manor, Whitworth Road, St Leonards-on-Sea, East Sussex, TN37 7PZ

The business was founded in 1924 by R.G. Rowland. Local bus operations started with an East Sussex County Council service between Bexhill and Hooe from 1980 to 1982. Since May 1986 Rambler has operated several journeys of the East Sussex County Rider scheme in the Battle and Bexhill areas, and from July 1987 took over a cross-Hastings service between St. Leonards and Hollington. In October 1990 this work was lost, but simultaneously a new Sunday service was gained covering part of the route and a commercial service began in Hastings. From September 1991 coastal route 44 between Hastings and Rye via Fairlight commenced under ESCC contract. In April 1994 Monday to Friday work on route 312 between Rye and Tenterden was gained.

Vehicles used on bus services carry a Ramblerbus name. An unusual recent acquisition was one of the four Bedford JJLs, the more remarkable for being the second time this vehicle had been in the fleet. A high-profile coaching operation continues to entail contract and private hire work, with the majority of coaches carrying private registrations from the former Hastings licensing office. Fleet livery is green, black and cream with pale green relief. The present garage was opened in May 1980, and the head office moved there in January 1990.

Most of Rambler's fleet originated from the municipal Maidstone fleet, finding its way to the coast by a variety of means. No.10 is a Bedford YMT with Wright TT bodywork which came through Maidstone & District as dealers, and was seen at Hastings Station in March 1993 on the coastal route to Rye via Fairlight. Terry Blackman

A most unusual vehicle is No.05, one of just four Bedford JJLs with Marshall bodywork to have been built. It had been in the Rambler fleet during the 1980s before passing to AWD for possible museum use, returning via dealers in the autumn of 1993. On 18th March 1994 it was seen in Hastings town centre on its second day back in service.
Terry Blackman

RAMBLER

01	LYC731	Bedford OB	Duple Vista	C29F	1950	Ex preservation, 1983
02	EDY565E	Bedford VAM14	Duple Viceroy	C45F	1967	Ex Plumridge, Horley, 1990
03	950KPE	Bedford YMQ	Duple Dominant II	C45F	1980	Ex Turner, Chulmleigh, 1984
05	HKX553X	Bedford JJL	Marshall	B24F	1979	Ex Holloway, Denham (npsv), 1993
06	PKO260W	Bedford YMT	Duple Dominant II	C53F	1981	Ex Moore & Verge, Cliftonville, 1992
10	CKN142Y	Bedford YMT	Wright TT	DP53F	1982	Ex Boro'line Maidstone, 1992
11	CKN143Y	Bedford YMT	Wright TT	DP53F	1982	Ex Boro'line Maidstone, 1992
12	MUY41X	Bedford YMQ	Wright TT	B45F	1982	Ex Perry, Bromyard, 1992
14	WNH52W	Bedford YMQS	Lex Maxeta	B33F	1981	Ex Milton Keynes City Bus, 1987
15	F609EHE	Mercedes-Benz 609D	Whittaker	C24F	1989	Ex Williams, St Albans, 1993
16	K16ADY	DAF Sherpa 400	Crystals	C16F	1992	
17	MDY397	Volvo B10M-61	Van Hool Alizée	C49FT	1988	Ex Excelsior, Bournemouth, 1993
18	LDY173	Volvo B10M-61	Van Hool Alizée	C51FT	1988	
19	SDY788	Volvo B10M-61	Van Hool Alizée	C53F	1987	Ex Shearings, Wigan, 1992
20	910OCV	Bedford YMT	Duple Dominant II	C53F	1977	Ex Coliseum, West End, 1990
21	ODY395	Bedford YNT	Plaxton Paramount 3200Exp	C53F	1984	Ex Sheffield United Transport, 1993
22	NCF715	Bedford YMT	Plaxton Supreme IV	C53F	1979	Ex Portrest, Southam, 1989
23	B929AAX	Bedford YNT	Plaxton Paramount 3200	C53F	1985	Ex Cleverly, Cwmbran, 1994
24	B930AAX	Bedford YNT	Plaxton Paramount 3200	C53F	1985	Ex Cleverly, Cwmbran, 1994
25	GDY493	Bedford YNT	Plaxton Paramount 3200	C51F	1984	Ex Hil-Tech, Hillingdon, 1993
26	8876FN	Bedford YNT	Plaxton Paramount 3200	C51F	1984	Ex Hil-Tech, Hillingdon, 1993
27	UDY512	Volvo B10M-60	Plaxton Paramount 3500 3	C51FT	1989	Ex Park, Hamilton, 1991
28	NDY820	Volvo B10M-60	Plaxton Paramount 3500 3	C51FT	1989	Ex Park, Hamilton, 1991
29	WUF44	Bedford YNT	Plaxton Paramount 3200	C53F	1983	Ex Hodson, Navenby, 1993
30	ODY607	Bedford YNT	Plaxton Paramount 3200	C53F	1984	Ex Associated, Worcester, 1993
31	1924RH	Bedford YNT	Plaxton Paramount 3200	C53F	1983	Ex Taylor, Meppershall, 1991
32	FDY83	Bedford YNT	Plaxton Paramount 3200	C53F	1984	Ex Barnes, Aldbourne, 1993
33	UDY910	Bedford YMPS	Plaxton Paramount 3200 3	C33F	1987	
34	RDY155	Bedford YMPS	Plaxton Paramount 3200 3	C33F	1987	
35	TDY388	Volvo B10M-60	Plaxton Paramount 3500 3	C51FT	1990	
36	KDY814	Volvo B10M-60	Plaxton Paramount 3500 3	C49FT	1991	Ex Wallace Arnold, Leeds, 1993
37	HDY405	Volvo B10M-61	Plaxton Paramount 3500 3	C53F	1987	
38	VDY468	Volvo B10M-60	Plaxton Paramount 3500 3	C53F	1991	Ex Wallace Arnold, Leeds, 1994
—	KWB695W	Bedford YMT	Duple Dominant	B55F	1981	Ex Rider (York), 1994

Previous registrations

FDY83	A440HJF
GDY493	A67NPP
HDY405	D137VJK
KDY814	H631UWR
LDY173	E184XJK
MDY397	AYU763 (Belgium), F450WFX, XEL941, F507MAA
MUY41X	ABH760X, 851PKJ
NCF715	YEB105T
NDY820	F28HGG
ODY395	A627YWF
ODY607	A383BNP
RDY155	D134VJK, TYW50
SDY788	D558MVR
TDY388	G135UWV
UDY512	F27HGG
UDY910	D133VJK
VDY468	H612UWR
WUF44	A244KFJ
8876FN	A68NPP
950KPE	ECB791W
910OCV	OTR412S
1924RH	JNM744Y, 617MUR, KUR585Y

RDH SERVICES

R.D. Hunnisett, 44 Dallas Lane, Barcombe, East Sussex, BN8 5DZ

RDH Services operates a number of East Sussex County Council contract services, using vehicles chiefly supplied from the County Council's stock of County Rider vehicles. Significant gains were achieved in the 1993 tendering round in the Lewes area. Amongst the mixed collection of vehicles is a Leyland Cub, a Leyland Swift and a Dennis Lancet, as well as a number of minibuses. A small coach fleet is also held for contract purposes.

Amongst the routes gained by RDH in the autumn 1993 round of East Sussex County Council tendering was the link from Tunbridge Wells to Groombridge replacing a former British Rail facility. D78TLV, a Freight Rover Sherpa with Carlyle conversion, had originated with London Country South West in 1987. David Harman

RDH SERVICES

Reg	Chassis	Body	Seating	Year	History
LAH800P	Mercedes-Benz LPO608	Duple	C29F	1975	Ex Thompson, Hillingdon, 1991
NWD755P	Ford R1114	Van Hool McArdle	C53F	1976	Ex Murphy, Rowlands Gill, 1988
YPL87T	AEC Reliance 6U2R	Duple Dominant Express	C53F	1979	Ex Smith, Bold Heath, 1993
OUF373W	MAN SR240	MAN	C53F	1981	Ex Jenkins, Seaford, 1992
PCD352X	Mercedes-Benz L508D	Pilcher-Greene	C18FL	1981	Ex Anthony House, Newhaven (npsv), 1988
FBP261X	Mercedes-Benz L508DG	Robin Hood	B16FL	1982	Ex Hailsham Town Bus, 1989
FNM740Y	Ford A0610	Mellor	B20F	1983	Ex Coachmaster, Coulsdon, 1988
KJK800Y	Leyland Cub CU335	Reeve Burgess	B24FL	1983	Ex East Sussex County Council, 1994
C28GKK	Leyland Cub CU335	Reeve Burgess	B30FL	1986	Ex East Sussex County Council, 1989
C277TDY	Dennis Lancet SDA524	Reeve Burgess	B30FL	1986	Ex East Sussex County Council, 1991
D78TLV	Freight Rover Sherpa 395D	Carlyle	B20F	1987	Ex London Country South West, 1990
D244OOJ	Freight Rover Sherpa 395D	Carlyle	B18F	1987	Ex Bee Line Buzz, Stockport, 1991
D199NON	Freight Rover Sherpa 395D	Carlyle	B18F	1987	Ex Bee Line Buzz, Stockport, 1991
D126WCC	Freight Rover Sherpa 395D	Carlyle	B18F	1987	Ex Mulpeter & Cutbush, Newhaven, 1993
F438OTP	Leyland Swift LBM6N/1RS	Wadham Stringer	B26FL	1988	Ex East Sussex County Council, 1992
H751DKL	Talbot Freeway	Talbot	B16F	1990	Ex East Sussex County Council, 1992

Previous registrations
OUF373W   NFJ375W, XS2210

READING BUSES

Reading Transport Ltd, Mill Lane, Reading, Berkshire, RG1 2RW

Reading Transport took over the operations of the Reading Borough Council Transport Department on 26th October 1986. It operated stage services within the borough boundaries and express services to and from London. Following the acquisition of the Reading and Newbury duties of The Bee Line in July 1992 the area of operation has increased.

The fleet remained stable during the latter half of the 1980s, but rapid updating has taken place since then with Leyland Olympians and youthful second-hand MCW Metrobuses from London Buses. Twelve Leyland Titans in the fleet represent the only significant purchase of the type as new in the South of England outside London. The single-deck fleet has been developed by the arrival of midibuses, and the coaching presence has been strengthened by the acquisition, in October 1991, of the London services of The Bee Line, together with some vehicles. Further vehicles came with The Bee Line operations in July 1992.

The new fleet livery of cream, burgundy and aquamarine (or green on Newbury-based buses) is now prevalent, although some examples remain of the traditional maroon and cream on white style. Vehicles on London services are in a three-tone blue livery. Vehicles are based at Mill Lane and Forbury in Reading and at Newbury.

Reading can always be relied upon to pursue an adventurous fleet policy. No.703 was the third of a trio of Optare Spectras purchased in 1992, more having followed since. Malcolm King

Amongst several Leyland Nationals which have found their way into the Reading fleet, No.344 had started life with Central SMT. It was photographed in Reading in September 1993. Colin Lloyd

Further innovative policies are evidenced by five Optare Vectas based on MAN chassis. One stands at Reading Station in September 1993. Colin Lloyd

Acquisition of the Newbury network of The Bee Line in 1992 brought with it three ageing Mercedes-Benz 609D minibuses with Robin Hood conversions. No.213 shows the localised fleetname applied to vehicles used on this operation. Malcolm King

---

READING TRANSPORT

11	E911DRD	Leyland Olympian ONLXB/1RH	Optare	H44/26D	1988	
12	E912DRD	Leyland Olympian ONLXB/1RH	Optare	H44/26D	1988	
13	E913DRD	Leyland Olympian ONLXB/1RH	Optare	H44/26D	1988	
14	E914DRD	Leyland Olympian ONLXB/1RH	Optare	H44/26D	1988	
15	E915DRD	Leyland Olympian ONLXCT/1RH	Optare	H44/26D	1988	
16	E916DRD	Leyland Olympian ONLXCT/1RH	Optare	H44/26D	1988	
17	E917DRD	Leyland Olympian ONLXB/1RH	Optare	H44/26D	1988	

70-74

	Leyland Titan TNLXB2RR	Leyland	H44/26D	1983

70	SBL70Y	71	RMO71Y	72	RMO72Y	73	RMO73Y	74	RMO74Y

75-79

	Leyland Titan TNLXC1RF	Leyland	DPH39/27F	1983

75	RMO75Y	76	RMO76Y	77	RMO77Y	78	RMO78Y	79	RMO79Y

82	D82UTF	Leyland Olympian ONLXCT/1RH	Eastern Coach Works	DPH39/25F	1986				
83	D83UTF	Leyland Olympian ONLXCT/1RH	Eastern Coach Works	DPH39/25F	1986				
84	D84UTF	Leyland Olympian ONLXCT/1RH	Eastern Coach Works	DPH39/25F	1986				
85	F85MJH	Leyland Olympian ONLXCT/1RH	Optare	DPH39/25F	1988				
86	F86MJH	Leyland Olympian ONLXCT/1RH	Optare	DPH39/25F	1988				
87	F87MJH	Leyland Olympian ONLXCT/1RH	Optare	DPH39/25F	1988				

143-149 MCW Metrobus 2 DR102/44 MCW DPH39/27F 1984

143	A143AMO	145	A145AMO	147	B147EDP	149	B149EDP
144	A144AMO	146	A146AMO	148	B148EDP		

150-165 MCW Metrobus DR102/8 MCW H43/27D 1979

150	WRD150T	154	WRD154T	158	WRD158T	162	WRD162T
151	WRD151T	155	WRD155T	159	WRD159T	163	WRD163T
152	WRD152T	156	WRD156T	160	WRD160T	164	CJH164V
153	WRD153T	157	WRD157T	161	WRD161T	165	CJH165V

166-183 MCW Metrobus DR102/16 MCW H45/27D 1980-81

166	CJH166V	171	CJH171V	176	HCF176W	181	HCF181W
167	CJH167V	172	CJH172V	177	HCF177W	182	HCF182W
168	CJH168V	173	HCF173W	178	HCF178W	183	HCF183W
169	CJH169V	174	HCF174W	179	HCF179W		
170	CJH170V	175	HCF175W	180	HCF180W		

184-188 MCW Metrobus DR102/25 MCW H45/28D 1982

184	LMO184X	185	LMO185X	186	LMO186X	187	LMO187X	188	LMO188X

189-193 MCW Metrobus DR102/30 MCW DPH43/25D 1982

189	LMO189X	190	LMO190X	191	LMO191X	192	LMO192X	193	LMO193X

201-210 Mercedes-Benz 811D Optare StarRider B26F 1988-89 Ex The Bee Line, 1992

201	F531NRD	203	F533NRD	205	F535NRD	207	F361SDP	209	F363SDP
202	F532NRD	204	F534NRD	206	F360SDP	208	F362SDP	210	F364SDP

211	E459CGM	Mercedes-Benz 609D	Robin Hood City Nippy	B20F	1987	Ex The Bee Line, 1992
212	E460CGM	Mercedes-Benz 609D	Robin Hood City Nippy	B20F	1987	Ex The Bee Line, 1992
213	E468CGM	Mercedes-Benz 609D	Robin Hood City Nippy	B20F	1987	Ex The Bee Line, 1992
214	D939KNW	Volkswagen LT55	Optare City Pacer	B25F	1986	Ex Lancaster, 1992
215	E236VUD	Volkswagen LT55	Optare City Pacer	B25F	1987	Ex Lancaster, 1992
216	WOI3005	MCW Metrorider MF154/1	MCW	DP26F	1989	Ex Ipswich, 1993
220	BUS5X	Scania K113CRB	Van Hool Alizée	C49FT	1989	
231	C912YPW	Hestair Duple 425	Duple 425	C55FT	1986	Ex Ambassador Travel, 1991
232	D124FDF	Hestair Duple 425	Duple 425	C55FT	1987	Ex Swanbrook, Cheltenham, 1991
233	E125LAD	Hestair Duple 425	Duple 425	C52FT	1988	Ex Swanbrook, Cheltenham, 1991

244-248 Hestair Duple 425 Duple 425 C55F 1987 Ex The Bee Line, 1991

244	E451CGM	245	E452CGM	246	E453CGM	247	E454CGM	248	E455CGM

251	K505RJX	DAF SB2700DHS585	Van Hool Alizée HE	C55F	1992	
252	J799KHD	DAF SB2700DHS585	Van Hool Alizée	C51F	1992	Ex demonstrator, 1992
261	G608SGU	Leyland Tiger TRCTL10/3ARZA	Plaxton Paramount 3200 3	C57F	1990	Ex London Buses, 1993
262	G100VMM	Leyland Tiger TRCTL10/3ARZA	Plaxton Paramount 3200 3	C57F	1990	Ex London Buses, 1993
306	LPB200P	Leyland National 10351/1R		DP39F	1976	Ex Eastbourne, 1992

307-319 Leyland National 1151/1R/0402 B49F 1973-74 Ex The Bee Line, 1992

307	NRD144M	308	NRD145M	314	NRD155M	318	NRD161M	319	NRD162M

322-343 Leyland National 11351/1R B49F 1974-75 Ex The Bee Line, 1992

322	TBL166M	333	GPC731N	339	GPJ895N	341	GPJ898N
332	GPC730N	334	GPC732N	340	GPJ896N	343	KPA355P

344	FNS162T	Leyland National 11351A/1R		B52F	1979	Ex Liyell, Ripley, 1992

345	KRE281P	Leyland National 11351/1R		B52F	1976	Ex PMT, 1993
346	KRE283P	Leyland National 11351/1R		B52F	1976	Ex PMT, 1993
347	OAE758R	Leyland National 11351A/2R		B49F	1977	Ex Bristol, 1993
358	NPJ483R	Leyland National 11351A/1R		B49F	1977	Ex The Bee Line, 1992
361	TPE147S	Leyland National 11351A/1R		B49F	1977	Ex The Bee Line, 1992
382	LPF603P	Leyland National 11351/1R/SC		B49F	1976	Ex The Bee Line, 1992
383	TPE171S	Leyland National 11351A/1R		B41F	1978	Ex The Bee Line, 1992

455-469   MCW Metrobus 2 DR102/63   MCW   H45/30F   1987   Ex London Buses, 1991

455	E454SON	458	E458SON	461	E247KCF	464	E464SON	467	E467SON
456	E456SON	459	E459SON	462	E462SON	465	E465SON	468	E468SON
457	E457SON	460	E460SON	463	E463SON	466	E466SON	469	E469SON

501-510   DAF SB220LC550   Optare Delta   B49F*   1989   * 508 is B44F

501	G501XBL	503	G503XBL	505	G505XBL	507	G507XBL	509	G509XBL
502	G502XBL	504	G504XBL	506	G506XBL	508	G508XBL	510	G510XBL

520-558   Bristol VRT/SL3/6LXB   Eastern Coach Works   H43/31F   1978-80 Ex The Bee Line, 1992

520	VPF285S	530	CJH116V	535	GGM77W	558	GGM79W
522	VPF287S	531	CJH118V	536	GGM78W		

562	SNJ590R	Bristol VRT/SL3/6LXB	Eastern Coach Works	H43/31F	1977	Ex Brighton & Hove, 1992
563	SNJ593R	Bristol VRT/SL3/6LXB	Eastern Coach Works	H43/31F	1977	Ex Brighton & Hove, 1992
564	CJH125V	Bristol VRT/SL3/6LXB	Eastern Coach Works	CH41/25F	1980	Ex The Bee Line, 1992
565	CJH126V	Bristol VRT/SL3/6LXB	Eastern Coach Works	CH41/25F	1980	Ex The Bee Line, 1992
573	RTH919S	Bristol VRT/SL3/501	Eastern Coach Works	H43/31F	1977	Ex The Bee Line, 1992
574	RTH921S	Bristol VRT/SL3/501	Eastern Coach Works	H43/31F	1977	Ex The Bee Line, 1992

601-606   MCW Metrorider MF158/8   MCW   B31F   1988

601	E601HTF	603	E603HTF	605	E605HTF
602	E602HTF	604	E603HTF	606	E606HTF

607-613   Optare Metrorider   Optare   B25F   1991

607	J607SJB	609	J609SJB	611	J611SPB	613	H613NJB
608	J608SJB	610	J610SJB	612	J612SPB		

701	MRD1	DAF DB250HS505	Optare Spectra	H43/28F	1992	
702	K702BBL	DAF DB250HS505	Optare Spectra	H43/28F	1992	
703	K703BBL	DAF DB250HS505	Optare Spectra	H43/28F	1992	
704	K170KYG	DAF DB250WB505	Optare Spectra	H46/28F	1992	Ex demonstrator, 1993
705	L705FRD	DAF DB250WS505	Optare Spectra	H46/28F	1994	
706	L706FRD	DAF DB250WS505	Optare Spectra	H46/28F	1994	
751	L751FRD	DAF DB250WS505	Optare Spectra	DPH37/25F	1993	
752	L752FRD	DAF DB250WS505	Optare Spectra	DPH37/25F	1994	
758	YPJ210Y	Leyland Tiger TRCTL11/3R	Plaxton Paramount 3500	C50F	1983	Ex The Bee Line, 1992
781	F771OJH	Volvo B10M-60	Jonckheere Jubilee P50	C53F	1989	Ex The Bee Line, 1992
784	F774OJH	Volvo B10M-60	Jonckheere Jubilee P50	C53F	1989	Ex The Bee Line, 1992
785	F755OJH	Volvo B10M-60	Jonckheere Jubilee P50	C53F	1989	Ex The Bee Line, 1992
801	K801DCF	MAN 11-180	Optare Vecta	B40F	1993	
802	K802DCF	MAN 11-180	Optare Vecta	B40F	1993	
803	K803DCF	MAN 11-190	Optare Vecta	B41F	1993	
804	K804DCF	MAN 11-190	Optare Vecta	B41F	1993	
805	K805DCF	MAN 11-190	Optare Vecta	B41F	1993	
806	L806FRD	MAN 11-190	Optare Vecta	B40F	1994	
807	L807FRD	MAN 11-190	Optare Vecta	B40F	1994	
808	L808FRD	MAN 11-190	Optare Vecta	B40F	1994	

Previous registrations
E247KCF   E475SON, MRD1
BUS5X   F220SDP

Special liveries
London link : 82/3, 244-8/51/2/61/2, 751/2/84
Overall advertisements : 11/5, 72/4, 87, 185, 530

READING MAINLINE

The Greater Reading Omnibus Co, PO Box 147, Reading, Berkshire, RG3 2XY

Reading Mainline started operations on 23rd July 1994, using Routemasters on cross-town routes from Tilehurst and Oxford Road to Whitley and Northumberland Avenue. The venture is headed by Mike Russell, formerly Operations Manager of Reading Transport. Just over a week after the start of the services Reading Transport fought back by introducing six new Metroliners running a few minutes ahead of the RMs.

The operating centre of Reading Mainline is at Cardiff Road, Reading, and vehicles are painted in red and cream livery.

READING MAINLINE

1	ALM34B	3	XVS319	5	WLT937	7	VLT44	9	WLT790
2	WLT993	4	ALM11B	6	WLT577	8	YTS973A	10	WYJ857

Previous registrations

XVS319	WLT949	WYJ857	VLT172
YTS973A	17CLT		

Reading Mainline No.3, one-time RM949, in Friar Street soon after entering service. As is often the case with operations managed by enthusiasts, a very attractive livery has been applied.
Russell Upcraft

RYE COACHES

Rye Coaches, 2 Simpson Industrial Park, Harbour Road, Rye, East Sussex, TN31 7ME

Rye Coaches entered local bus operation in October 1990 when the Monday to Friday contract for East Sussex County Council route 312 between Rye and Tenterden was gained together with occasional journeys on other rural routes. Further work was acquired subsequently. During the summer of 1993 control of the firm passed to the Warren, Ticehurst group, and the Rye depot was closed in March 1994. Vehicles moved to Ticehurst, although the Rye address is still used for formal purposes. Following this move, operations are now restricted to Tuesday route 24 from Rye to Maidstone and Friday route 293 from Rye via Appledore to Tenterden. The fleet is gradually being repainted into Warren colours of yellow with Prussian blue and red relief.

RYE COACHES

NWO491R	Leyland National 11351A/1R		B52F	1976	Ex White-Hide & Bowen, Rye, 1993
CWG757V	Leyland Atlantean AN68A/1R	Roe	H45/29D	1979	Ex White-Hide & Bowen, Rye, 1993
VPR938	Volvo B10M-61	Duple Dominant IV	C48FT	1981	Ex White-Hide & Bowen, Rye, 1993
CNH175X	Leyland Leopard PSU3G/4RT	Eastern Coach Works B51	C49F	1982	Ex White-Hide & Bowen, Rye, 1993
E693WNE	Talbot Express	Made to Measure	C14F	1988	Ex Warren, Tenterden, 1994
KBZ2276	Volvo B10M	Plaxton Paramount 3500 3	C53F	——	Ex untraced owner, 1994

Previous registrations
KBZ2276   not traced
VPR938   XNV93W, XYN591, WRP226W

The smart grey and blue livery of Rye Coaches is now being replaced by the colours of the Warren group following their purchase of the operation in 1993. Leyland National NWO491R stands at Tenterden Town Hall in front of the Tudor Rose tearooms; the Rye route has since passed to Rambler Coaches. Alan Simpkins

SAFEGUARD

Safeguard Coaches Ltd, Friary Bus Station, Commercial Road, Guildford, Surrey, GU2 5TH

The fleet originated in a charabanc operation started in 1924 by Arthur Newman, a local coal merchant and haulier. A stage service in Guildford commenced in 1927.

For many years Safeguard pursued a vehicle policy based on the locally-produced Dennis chassis, though the current fleet is epitomised by Leylands and Volvos, together with two Dennis Darts. Farnham Coaches was acquired in 1988 together with a fleet of Setras, and other vehicles have since been repainted into Farnham Coaches livery, gaining private index marks. In addition to local services, the company operates a local bus service between Aldershot and Camberley during the week and school services in the surrounding areas.

The bus livery is dark red and cream, while coaches are painted cream, red and grey. The garage is at Ridgemount Garage, Guildford Park. Farnham Coaches vehicles are kept at Odiham Road, Ewshot, Farnham.

SAFEGUARD

KUS244Y	Leyland Tiger TRBTL11/2R	Duple Dominant	B53F	1982	Ex Hutchison, Overtown, 1986
515FCG	Kässbohrer Setra S215H	Kässbohrer Rational	C53F	1982	Ex Farnham Coaches, 1988
247FCG	Kässbohrer Setra S215HD	Kässbohrer Tornado	C49FT	1983	Ex Farnham Coaches, 1988
531FCG	Kässbohrer Setra S215HD	Kässbohrer Tornado	C49FT	1983	Ex Farnham Coaches, 1988
A60GPL	Mercedes-Benz L608D	Reeve Burgess	C19F	1984	
A62HPG	Leyland Tiger TRCTL11/3R	Plaxton Paramount 3200	C53F	1984	
B906SPR	Volvo B10M-61	Plaxton Paramount 3200 2	C53F	1984	Ex Excelsior, Bournemouth, 1987
B907SPR	Volvo B10M-61	Plaxton Paramount 3200 2	C53F	1984	Ex Excelsior, Bournemouth, 1986
277FCG	Kässbohrer Setra S215HR	Kässbohrer Rational	C53F	1984	Ex Farnham Coaches, 1988
C164SPB	Leyland Tiger TRBTL11/2R	Duple Dominant	B53F	1985	
538FCG	Kässbohrer Setra S215HR	Kässbohrer Rational	C49FT	1986	Ex Tourswift, Birtley, 1990
C105AFX	Volvo B10M-61	Plaxton Paramount 3200 2	C53F	1986	Ex Excelsior, Bournemouth, 1987
D123HML	Mercedes-Benz L608D	Reeve Burgess	C19F	1986	
D159HML	Mercedes-Benz 609D	Reeve Burgess	B20F	1986	
D633XVV	Volkswagen LT55	Optare CityPacer	B25F	1986	Ex Leicester, 1991
D165HML	Leyland Lynx LX112TL11FR1	Leyland	B49F	1987	
E51MMT	Leyland Lynx LX112TL11FR1S	Leyland	B49F	1987	
159FCG	Kässbohrer Setra S215HD	Kässbohrer Tornado	C47FT	1987	Ex Farnham Coaches, 1988
E297OMG	Leyland Lynx LX112L10ZR1R	Leyland	B49F	1988	
E298OMG	Leyland Lynx LX112L10ZR1R	Leyland	B49F	1988	
F296RMH	Volvo B10M-46	Plaxton Paramount 3200 3	C39F	1988	
F474WFX	Volvo B10M-60	Plaxton Paramount 3200 3	C53F	1989	Ex Excelsior, Bournemouth, 1989
196FCG	Volvo B10M-60	Plaxton Paramount 3200 3	C53F	1989	Ex Excelsior, Bournemouth, 1989
F624CWJ	Auwaerter Neoplan N122/3	Auwaerter Skyliner	CH57/20DT	1989	Ex Stockdale, Selby, 1993
DSK558	Volvo B10M-60	Plaxton Paramount 3500 3	C53F	1989	Ex Wallace Arnold, 1992
G122KUB	Mercedes-Benz 811D	Optare StarRider	C29F	1989	Ex Brents, Watford, 1993
DSK559	Volvo B10M-60	Plaxton Paramount 3500 3	C53F	1990	Ex Wallace Arnold, 1993
G514EFX	Volvo B10M-60	Plaxton Paramount 3200 3	C53F	1990	Ex Excelsior, Bournemouth, 1991
G520EFX	Volvo B10M-60	Plaxton Paramount 3200 3	C57F	1990	Ex Excelsior, Bournemouth, 1991
DSK560	Volvo B10M-60	Plaxton Paramount 3500 3	C53F	1990	Ex Wallace Arnold, 1993
H672ATN	Toyota HB31R	Caetano Optimo II	C21F	1990	Ex Rose, Broadway, 1992
K628YPL	Dennis Dart 9.8SDL	Plaxton Pointer	B40F	1993	
L265EPD	Dennis Dart 9.8SDL3035	Plaxton Pointer	B40F	1994	

Previous registrations

DSK558	F437DUG	247FCG	RAX22Y
DSK559	G540LWU	515FCG	UPB669X
DSK560	G515LWU	531FCG	APA672Y
196FCG	F475WFX	538FCG	C665UPJ, DSK559

Special liveries
Farnham Coaches B906SPR, D123HML, C105AFX, F624CWJ
Globus Gateway 247FCG, 531FCG

SMITH'S

W.H.V. and Mrs V. Smith, 59 Staplehurst Road, Sittingbourne, Kent, ME10 2NY

Following the relaxation of licensing regulations in October 1980, Smith's Coaches started a commuter service between Sheerness, Sittingbourne and London. Local bus operations started in the spring of 1986 when a pre-deregulation pilot batch of tenders was sought by Kent County Council. Leyland Nationals were purchased in 1987 to replace the original bus-grant Ford coaches. In November 1989 Smith's Coaches stepped in to take over the Kent County Council routes between Sheerness and Sittingbourne surrendered by Lambkin Coaches and also commenced a weekday evening contract operation of local services on the Isle of Sheppey, though these were lost in April 1994. Market-day services to Maidstone and Canterbury also form part of the profile.

Most vehicles are in grey, black and white (some also with red) and the fleet is based at the licensed address.

Smith's continue to work their original group of routes to villages around Sittingbourne, on which Leyland Nationals have replaced the earlier bus grant Ford coaches. Former London Buses THX143S passes near the Staplehurst Road garage in July 1993. Nicholas King

SMITH'S

Reg	Type	Body		Seats	Year	Notes
JG9938	Leyland Tiger TS8	Park Royal		C32F	1937	Ex preservation, 1988
ODL885R	Leyland National 10351A/1R			B44F	1977	Ex Southern Vectis, 1987
ODL888R	Leyland National 10351A/1R			B44F	1977	Ex Southern Vectis, 1987
THX143S	Leyland National 10351A/2R			B36D	1978	Ex London Buses, 1990
AKL640T	Ford R1114	Duple Dominant II Express	C53F		1978	
JFD288V	Ford R1114	Duple Dominant II		C53F	1979	Ex Olsen, Strood, 1980
OHA467W	Ford R1114	Plaxton Supreme IV		C53F	1980	Ex Parry, Cheslyn Hay, 1982
A638LKO	Ward Dalesman TV8-640	Plaxton Paramount 3200	C57F		1983	
LIB7133	Leyland Tiger TRCTL11/3R	Plaxton Paramount 3500	C53F		1984	Ex Hills, Tredegar, 1988
LIB7134	Leyland Tiger TRCTL11/3R	Plaxton Paramount 3500	C53F		1984	Ex Hills, Tredegar, 1988
B164TKL	Leyland Tiger TRCTL11/3R	Plaxton Paramount 3200	C57F		1984	
B46XKJ	Leyland Tiger TRCTL11/3R	Plaxton Paramount 3500	C53F		1985	
MIB526	Leyland Royal Tiger RTC	Leyland Doyen		C48FT	1986	Ex Fishwick, Leyland, 1988
D330NTG	Leyland Tiger TRCTL11/3RZ	Jonckheere Jubilee P599	C51FT		1986	Ex Thomas, Clydach Vale, 1992
E720VKE	Talbot Express	Crystals		C14F	1987	
E75VKO	Leyland Tiger TRCTL11/3RZ	Plaxton Paramount 3200 3	C57F		1987	
E76VKO	Leyland Tiger TRCTL11/3RZ	Plaxton Paramount 3200 3	C57F		1987	
F337JTN	Toyota HB31R	Caetano Optimo		C21F	1988	Ex Proctor, Bedale, 1993
F22YBO	Kässbohrer Setra S215HDI	Kässbohrer Tornado		C49FT	1989	Ex Bebb, Llantwit Fardre, 1991
G957WNR	Dennis Javelin 12SDA1907	Plaxton Paramount 3200 3	C57F		1990	Ex Reliance, Gravesend, 1993
G958WNR	Dennis Javelin 12SDA1907	Plaxton Paramount 3200 3	C57F		1990	Ex Reliance, Gravesend, 1993

Previous registrations

LIB7133	A782WHB		MIB526	C752MFR
LIB7134	A586WNY		D330NTG	C335HHB

Named vehicle
F22YBO Pride of Swale

SOUTHAMPTON CITYBUS

Southampton City Transport (1993) Ltd, 226 Portswood Road, Southampton, Hants, SO9 4XS

This company was established on 21st December 1993 in succession to Southampton Citybus Ltd, itself formed to take over the former municipal operations in October 1986. The traditional operating area is bounded by the M27 to the north, Totton in the west and Hedge End in the east, though the operation of Hampshire County Council services and several commercial services result in vehicles appearing some way outside this boundary. Competition has also been experienced from Solent Blue Line on services within Southampton and a fleet of crew-operated Routemasters was for a while operated to counteract this. Services were introduced in Portsmouth under the Red Admiral name, though this has since passed to Transit Holdings.

Fleet livery is red with a black skirt; most coaches are in overall red under the 'Red Ensign' name. Almost all buses are named.

Increased fleet requirements at Southampton in 1992 led to the arrival of a number of elderly Leyland Atlanteans with Roe bodywork from Plymouth. Several have already been withdrawn; No.125 is one of those to have survived.

A number of Dennis Darts have been taken into stock for single-deck requirements. No.307 was bought in 1990 from Wadham Stringer, for whom it had acted as a demonstrator. Malcolm King

Five older Leyland Atlanteans had enough life left in them to be rebodied as single-deckers by East Lancs in 1991, receiving age-disguising registrations shortly afterwards. No.351 typifies this unusual exercise. Malcolm McDonald

Coaching operations are carried out under the Red Ensign banner. Amongst four Leyland Olympians with East Lancs coachwork which parade in this form is No.503.

Among the oldest examples of significant numbers of AN68 Atlanteans with East Lancs bodies in the Southampton fleet is No.169, delivered in 1972.

SOUTHAMPTON CITYBUS

102	F102RTR	Leyland Lynx LX112L10ZR1S	Leyland		B47F	1989			
104-111		Leyland Lynx LX2R11C15ZR4	Leyland		B47F	1990			
104	G104WRV	**106**	G106WRV	**108**	G108WRV	**110**	G110XOW		
105	G105WRV	**107**	G107WRV	**109**	G109XOW	**111**	G111XOW		
112	G112XOW	Leyland Lynx LX112L10ZR1R	Leyland		DP47F	1990			
113	G113XOW	Leyland Lynx LX112L10ZR1R	Leyland		DP47F	1990			
114	K114DRV	Volvo B10B-58	Northern Counties						
			Countybus Paladin		B51F	1993			
119	OCO119S	Leyland Atlantean AN68A/1R	Roe		H43/28F	1978	Ex Plymouth, 1992		
124-128		Leyland Atlantean AN68A/1R	Roe		H43/28F	1979	Ex Plymouth, 1992		
124	STK124T	**125**	STK125T	**126**	STK126T	**127**	STK127T	**128**	STK128T
133	TTR167H	Leyland Atlantean PDR1A/1	East Lancs		H43/13FL	1970			
134	TTR168H	Leyland Atlantean PDR1A/1	East Lancs		H43/13FL	1970			

168-200
Leyland Atlantean AN68/1R East Lancs H45/31F 1972-75

168	EOW401L	178	PCR301M	188	HTR558P	192	HTR562P	196	HTR565P
169	EOW402L	182	PCR305M	189	HTR559P	193	HTR563P	197	HRT566P
172	PCR295M	183	PCR306M	190	HTR560P	194	HTR564P	200	HRT569P
174	PCR297M	184	PCR307M	191	HTR561P	195	HTR557P		

232-261
Leyland Atlantean AN68A/1R East Lancs H45/31F 1979-80

232	UPO232T	239	UPO239T	246	UPO246T	253	YRV253V	260	YRV260V
233	UPO233T	240	UPO240T	247	YRV247V	254	YRV254V	261	YRV261V
234	UPO234T	241	UPO241T	248	YRV248V	255	YRV255V		
235	UPO235T	242	UPO242T	249	YRV249V	256	YRV256V		
236	UPO236T	243	UPO243T	250	YRV250V	257	YRV257V		
237	UPO237T	244	UPO244T	251	YRV251V	258	YRV258V		
238	UPO238T	245	UPO245T	252	YRV252V	259	YRV259V		

262-266
Leyland Atlantean AN68B/1R East Lancs H45/31F 1981

262	DBK262W	263	DBK263W	264	DBK264W	265	DBK265W	266	DBK266W

267-276
Leyland Atlantean AN68C/1R East Lancs H45/31F* 1982 * 270/3/4 are H40/31F

267	FTR267X	269	FTR269X	271	FTR271X	273	KOW273Y	275	KOW275Y
268	FTR268X	270	FTR270X	272	KOW272Y	274	KOW274Y	276	KOW276Y

277	A277ROW	Dennis Dominator DDA171	East Lancs	H46/30F	1984	
289	E289HRV	Leyland Olympian ONLXB/1RH	Eastern Coach Works	DPH43/27F	1987	
290	E290HRV	Leyland Olympian ONLXB/1RH	Eastern Coach Works	DPH43/27F	1987	

301-306
Dennis Dart 9SDL3002 Duple Dartline B36F* 1990 * 306 is B35F

301	G301XCR	303	G303XCR	305	G305XCR
302	G302XCR	304	G304XCR	306	G306XCR

307	G895XPX	Dennis Dart 8.5SDL3003	Wadham Stringer Portsdown	B33F	1990	Ex demonstrator, 1990
308	H308ERV	Dennis Dart 9SDL3002	Reeve Burgess Pointer	B35F	1991	

309-313
Dennis Dart 9SDL3011 Plaxton Pointer B35F 1993

309	L309RTP	310	L310RTP	311	L311RTP	312	L312RTP	313	L313RTP

350-354
Leyland Atlantean AN68/1R East Lancs Sprint (1991) B35F 1974

350	OJI1870	351	OJI1871	352	OJI1879	353	OJI1873	354	OJI1874

498	709LAU	Scania K112TRS	Berkhof Emperor 395	CH57/19CT	1985	Ex Thamesdown, 1993
499	DSU405	Kässbohrer Setra S228DT	Kässbohrer Imperial	CH54/20CT	1984	Ex Ron, Ashington, 1993
500	115CLT	Kässbohrer Setra S228DT	Kässbohrer Imperial	CH54/20CT	1984	Ex Harris, Catshill, 1991
501	MJI4605	Kässbohrer Setra S228DT	Kässbohrer Imperial	CH55/20CT	1984	Ex Smith, Bold Heath, 1992
502	SIB3272	Leyland Olympian ONLXCT/2R	East Lancs	CH47/21F	1986	
503	SIB3273	Leyland Olympian ONLXCT/2R	East Lancs	CH47/29F	1986	
504	WLT649	Leyland Olympian ONTL11/2Rsp	East Lancs	CH49/20FT	1986	Ex London Coaches, 1990
505	SIB3275	Leyland Olympian ONTL11/2Rsp	East Lancs	CH49/20FT	1986	Ex London Coaches, 1990
507	WOW529J	Leyland Atlantean PDR1A/1	East Lancs	O45/31F	1971	
A1	C541BHY	Ford Transit	Dormobile	B14F	1986	Ex Badgerline, 1994
A2	C502BFB	Ford Transit	Dormobile	B14F	1985	Ex Badgerline, 1994

Previous registrations

DSU405	A414GPY	SIB3272	C287BBP
MJI4605	A574GEF	SIB3273	C288BBP
OJI1870	PCR299M	SIB3275	C202DYE
OJI1871	HTR567P	WLT649	C201DYE
OJI1873	HTR570P	115CLT	B149NPE, SWH67
OJI1874	HTR568P	709LAU	C276GVX
OJI1879	EOW398L		

Almost all vehicles in the fleet carry names

SOUTHERN VECTIS / SOLENT BLUE LINE

Southern Vectis Omnibus Company Ltd, Nelson Road, Newport, Isle of Wight, PO30 1RD
Musterphantom Ltd, 16 Stoneham Lane, Swaythling, Southampton, Hampshire

Southern Vectis was formed in 1929 when the Southern Railway Company took over the business of Dodson Brothers Ltd, trading as 'Vectis'. The name therefore reflects the original ownership rather than geographical confinement to the south of the island. Services expanded and many smaller stage and tour operators were acquired over the years until a near-monopoly of services was achieved. The company was nationalised in 1948 and passed to the National Bus Company in 1969. In October 1986 it became the third of the NBC's subsidiaries to be sold when it was purchased by a management team. Further expansion took place in 1987 when the West Wight fleet, comprising four coaches, was acquired.

Expansion of a different kind took place in September 1987 when Southern Vectis, acting in conjunction with Badgerline, set up 'Badger Vectis' to compete with Wilts & Dorset on the Bournemouth to Poole corridor, though this operation ceased in March 1988.

The Southern Vectis and Solent Blue Line fleets are treated as one combined unit, though interchange is fairly rare. A notable feature is the development of a fleet of veteran vehicles operating on the Isle of Wight in their original liveries. The current Southern Vectis fleet livery is emerald green and greensand for buses, with silver grey for coaches. Minibuses are in red or blue. Vehicles are based at Newport, Ryde, Freshwater, Sandown, Ventnor and East Cowes. The Solent Blue Line fleet operates in a diagonally-structured livery of yellow and two blues, and is based at depots in Southampton, Eastleigh and Hythe.

In common with many other operators, Southern Vectis moved to Northern Counties for bodywork on its Leyland Olympians after the Leyland bodyshop closed. No.742 is one of nine new in 1993 with coach seating for dedicated use on the Island Explorer service. Alan Simpkins

A collection of vintage Bristol vehicles has been assembled by Southern Vectis, each of them operating in a distinctive livery. The oldest bus still in regular service in the south of England, No.502 is a Bristol K5G of 1939 with Eastern Coach Works body. Known as "The Old Girl", this remarkable machine carries a full upper-deck load past Alum Bay in June 1993. Tony Wilson

Equally distinguished is No.501, a Bristol LD6G of 1956 also with Eastern Coach Works body on the summer open-top service between Ryde and Alum Bay. Malcolm King

No.611, painted in Tilling green livery, is a Bristol FLF6G with forward-entrance Eastern Coach Works body. Dating from 1965, it was re-acquired from Shamrock & Rambler in 1986. P.J. Relf

Relatively few standard Bristol VRTs survive on the island, Leyland Olympians having ousted them on most workings. No.671 approaches the town centre in Newport. P.J. Relf

Leyland Olympians taken into the fleet at the turn of the decade were fitted with dual-purpose seating and equipped with five-speed gearboxes. No.723 is one such vehicle. P.J. Relf

An unusual order received in 1992 was for eight Iveco Daily vehicles with bodies by Car Chairs. No.238 passes along Ryde Esplanade in the course of working a local town service. P.J. Relf

The first minibuses arrived on the Isle of Wight in 1985 in the form of Ford Transits. Later in the decade the preferred type was the Iveco Daily with Robin Hood body conversion. Malcolm King

A VRT allocated to the Solent Blue Line fleet is followed in this view by a Leyland National, the latter type in process of withdrawal. Malcolm King

No.721 is also allocated to the Solent Blue Line fleet. The naming of certain vehicles in this fleet will be noted both on the subject and on its immediate sister behind it. Malcolm King

SOUTHERN VECTIS/SOLENT BLUE LINE

83	NDL653R	Bristol VRT/SL3/6LXB	Eastern Coach Works	H43/31F	1977	
84	NDL654R	Bristol VRT/SL3/6LXB	Eastern Coach Works	H43/31F	1977	
85	RPR715R	Bristol VRT/SL3/6LXB	Eastern Coach Works	H43/31F	1977	Ex Hampshire Bus, 1987
87	RPR717R	Bristol VRT/SL3/6LXB	Eastern Coach Works	H43/31F	1977	Ex Hampshire Bus, 1987
89	VPR489S	Bristol VRT/SL3/6LXB	Eastern Coach Works	H43/31F	1977	Ex Hampshire Bus, 1987
94	RFB614S	Bristol VRT/SL3/6LXB	Eastern Coach Works	H43/31F	1978	
95	VOD595S	Bristol VRT/SL3/6LXB	Eastern Coach Works	H43/31F	1978	Ex Devon General, 1987
96	BFX576T	Bristol VRT/SL3/6LXB	Eastern Coach Works	H43/31F	1979	Ex Hampshire Bus, 1987
97	BFX577T	Bristol VRT/SL3/6LXB	Eastern Coach Works	H43/31F	1979	Ex Hampshire Bus, 1987
98	PTT98R	Bristol VRT/SL3/6LXB	Eastern Coach Works	H43/31F	1977	Ex Devon General, 1987

100-107

	Bristol VRT/SL3/6LXB	Eastern Coach Works	H43/31F	1977

100	ODL660R	102	ODL662R	104	ODL664R	106	ODL666R
101	ODL661R	103	ODL663R	105	ODL665R	107	ODL667R

149-164

	Bristol VRT/SL3/501	Eastern Coach Works	H43/31F	1978-79 Ex Cumberland, 1987
		Modified to Gardner 6LXB engines		

149	LHG449T	153	LHG453T	157	LHG457T	161	TRN461V
150	LHG450T	154	LHG454T	158	LHG458T	162	TRN462V
151	LHG451T	155	LHG455T	159	LHG459T	163	TRN463V
152	LHG452T	156	LHG456T	160	TRN460V	164	TRN464V

202	KDL202W	Bristol LHS6L	Eastern Coach Works	DP31F	1980
203	KDL203W	Bristol LHS6L	Eastern Coach Works	DP31F	1980

205-212 Mercedes-Benz 811D   Phoenix   B31F   1990

205	G205YDL	207	G207YDL	209	G209YDL	211	G211YDL
206	G206YDL	208	G208YDL	210	G210YDL	212	G212YDL

224	C224SRU	Ford Transit 190D	Robin Hood	B16F	1985	Ex Hampshire Bus, 1987
225	C225SRU	Ford Transit 190D	Robin Hood	B16F	1985	Ex Hampshire Bus, 1987
226	C226SRU	Ford Transit 190D	Robin Hood	B16F	1985	Ex Hampshire Bus, 1987

231-238 Iveco Daily 49.10   Car Chairs   B23F   1992

231	J231KDL	233	J233KDL	235	J235KDL	237	J237KDL
232	J232KDL	234	J234KDL	236	J236KDL	238	J238KDL

253-268 Ford Transit 190D   Carlyle   B16F*   1985   * 262 is C16F

253	C253SDL	263	C263SDL	265	C265SDL	267	C267SDL
262	WXI6291	264	C264SDL	266	C266SDL	268	C268SDL

269	D269YDL	Ford Transit 190D	Dormobile	DP18F	1986	
270	D270YDL	Ford Transit 190D	Dormobile	B18F	1986	

271-287 Iveco Daily 49.10   Robin Hood City Nippy   B19F   1987-89

271	E271HDL	275	E275HDL	279	E279HDL	283	F283ODL	287	F287ODL
272	E272HDL	276	E276HDL	280	F280ODL	284	F284ODL		
273	E273HDL	277	E277HDL	281	F281ODL	285	F285ODL		
274	E274HDL	278	E278HDL	282	F282ODL	286	F286ODL		

288	G565YTR	Iveco Daily 49.10	Phoenix	B23F	1990	Ex demonstrator, 1990
289	H289DDL	Iveco Daily 49.10	Phoenix	B23F	1990	
301	KDL885F	Bristol RESH6G	Duple Commander	C45F	1968	
302	CXI5971	Leyland Leopard PSU3C/4R	Plaxton Supreme IV Exp	C52F	1979	Ex The Bee Line, 1989
307	LXI4409	Leyland Leopard PSU3F/4R	Plaxton Supreme IV	C53F	1981	
310	WDL142	Leyland Tiger TRCTL11/3R	Plaxton Paramount 3200	C51F	1983	
311	WDL311Y	Leyland Tiger TRCTL11/3R	Plaxton Paramount 3200	C51F	1983	
312	A312BOL	Leyland Tiger TRCTL11/3R	Plaxton Paramount 3200	C51F	1984	
313	A313BOL	Leyland Tiger TRCTL11/3R	Plaxton Paramount 3200	C51F	1984	
314	WDL748	Leyland Tiger TRCTL11/3R	Plaxton Paramount 3200 2	C45FT	1986	
315	473CDL	Leyland Tiger TRCTL11/3R	Plaxton Paramount 3200 2	C51F	1986	
316	390CDL	Leyland Tiger TRCTL11/3R	Plaxton Paramount 3200 2	C47F	1986	
317	LBZ3474	Leyland Tiger TRCTL11/3R	Plaxton Paramount 3500 2	C51F	1986	
320	E320JDL	Leyland Tiger TRCTL11/3RZ	Plaxton Paramount 3500 3	C53F	1988	
321	E321JDL	Leyland Tiger TRCTL11/3RZ	Plaxton Paramount 3500 3	C53F	1988	
326	934BDL	Leyland Tiger TRCTL11/3R	Plaxton Paramount 3200	C53F	1984	Ex Hill, Tredegar, 1989

417-423 Leyland National 11351A/1R   B49F   1977-78 Ex Hampshire Bus, 1987
(422 is DP48F)

417	UFX852S	419	VFX985S	421	DRU7T	423	FPR65V
418	VFX982X	420	WPR150S	422	FPR64V		

500	MDL955	Bristol LD6G	Eastern Coach Works	O33/27R	1956	Ex preservation, 1993
501	MDL952	Bristol LD6G	Eastern Coach Works	O33/27R	1956	
502	CDL899	Bristol K5G	Eastern Coach Works	O30/26R	1939	
503	VDL613S	Bristol VRT/SL3/6LXB	Eastern Coach Works	CO43/31F	1977	Ex Hants & Dorset, 1979
504	UFX856S	Bristol VRT/SL3/6LXB	Eastern Coach Works	CO43/31F	1977	Ex Hants & Dorset, 1979
505	UFX857S	Bristol VRT/SL3/6LXB	Eastern Coach Works	CO43/31F	1977	Ex Hants & Dorset, 1979
506	UFX858S	Bristol VRT/SL3/6LXB	Eastern Coach Works	CO43/31F	1977	Ex Hants & Dorset, 1979
511	L526YDL	Volvo B10B-58	Alexander	B47F	1994	
512	L527YDL	Volvo B10B-58	Alexander	B47F	1994	
513	L528YDL	Volvo B10B-58	Alexander	B47F	1994	
514	L227THP	Volvo B10B-58	Alexander	B47F	1994	Ex Volvo Bus, Lanark, 1994
563	SDL268	Bristol LD6G	Eastern Coach Works	H33/27R	1959	Ex preservation, 1980
565	TDL998	Bristol FS6G	Eastern Coach Works	H33/27RD	1960	
573	YDL318	Bristol FS6G	Eastern Coach Works	H33/27RD	1962	
611	CDL479C	Bristol FLF6G	Eastern Coach Works	H38/32F	1965	Ex Shamrock & Rambler, 1986
628	SDL638J	Bristol VRT/SL2/6LX	Eastern Coach Works	H39/31F	1971	
668	UDL668S	Bristol VRT/SL3/6LXB	Eastern Coach Works	H43/31F	1978	
669	UDL669S	Bristol VRT/SL3/6LXB	Eastern Coach Works	H43/31F	1978	
670	UDL670S	Bristol VRT/SL3/6LXB	Eastern Coach Works	H43/31F	1978	

671-685 — Bristol VRT/SL3/6LXB — Eastern Coach Works — H43/31F — 1979-81

671	YDL671T	674	YDL674T	677	FDL677V	680	FDL680V	683	FDL683V
672	YDL672T	675	YDL675T	678	FDL678V	681	FDL681V	684	FDL684V
673	YDL673T	676	YDL676T	679	FDL679V	682	FDL682V	685	FDL685V

686-700 — Leyland Olympian ONLXB/1R — Eastern Coach Works — H45/30F — 1982-84

686	RDL686X	689	RDL689X	692	RDL692X	695	WDL695Y	698	A698DDL
687	RDL687X	690	RDL690X	693	WDL693Y	696	WDL696Y	699	A699DDL
688	RDL688X	691	RDL691X	694	WDL694Y	697	A697DDL	700	A700DDL

695	A295FDL	Leyland Olympian ONLXB/1R	Eastern Coach Works	DPH41/32F	1984

701-705 — Leyland Olympian ONLXB/1R — Eastern Coach Works — H45/30F — 1982 — Ex Hampshire Bus, 1987

701	A201MEL	702	A202MEL	703	A203MEL	704	A204MEL	705	A205MEL

706-712 — Leyland Olympian ONCL10/1RZ — Leyland — DPH39/29F — 1989

706	F706SDL	708	F708SDL	710	F710SDL	712	F712SDL
707	F707SDL	709	F709SDL	711	F711SDL		

713-727 — Leyland Olympian ON2R50C13Z5 — Leyland — DPH41/29F* 1989-90 * 717/9-22/4/7 are DPH43/29F

713	G713WDL	716	G716WDL	719	G719WDL	722	G722WDL	725	G725XDL
714	G714WDL	717	G717WDL	720	G720WDL	723	G723XDL	726	G726XDL
715	G715WDL	718	G718WDL	721	G721WDL	724	G724XDL	727	G727XDL

728-734 — Leyland Olympian ON2R50C13Z5 — Leyland — H47/31F — 1991

728	H728DDL	730	H730DDL	732	H732DDL	734	H734DDL
729	H729DDL	731	H731DDL	733	H733DDL		

735-743 — Leyland Olympian ON2R50C13Z4 Northern Counties Countybus Palatine — DPH41/29F 1993

735	K735ODL	737	K737ODL	739	K739ODL	741	K741ODL	743	K743ODL
736	K736ODL	738	K738ODL	740	K740ODL	742	K742ODL		

806	FDL927D	Bristol MW6G	Eastern Coach Works	B45F	1966	Ex preservation, 1989
817	F817URN	Leyland Olympian ONCL10/1RZ	Leyland	H47/31F	1988	Ex demonstrator, 1990
863	TDL563K	Bristol RELL6G	Eastern Coach Works	B53F	1971	
901	H901EDL	Kässbohrer Setra S215HD	Kässbohrer Tornado	C49F	1991	
902	J902LDL	Kässbohrer Setra S215HD	Kässbohrer Tornado	C47F	1992	

Previous registrations

CXI5971	WJM811T
LDZ3474	C317TDL
LXI4409	RDL307X
TDL998	TDL998, ABK832A
VDL613S	UFX855S, 473CDL
WDL142	WDL310Y
WDL748	C314TDL
WXI6291	C262SDL
934BDL	A780WHB
390CDL	C316TDL
473CDL	C315TDL
A295DFL	A702DDL, WDL142

Special liveries
Overall advertisements : 83/5/9, 155/7, 285, 419, 501/4, 679/83/91/3, 728
Tilling : 301, 563/5/73, 611/28, 806/63

Named vehicles
89 Nick Girder, 149 Southampton Mencap, 150 Wendy Knight, 154 T S Astrid, 155 Josie Nicholls, 160 Eileen Howlett, 161 British Diabetic Assn, Southampton, 162 RSPCA Action for Animals, 163 Romsey Lions, 164 Mary Hill, 721 Southampton-le Havre Twinning Society, 722 Southampton Mind Crisis

STAGECOACH SOUTH

Stagecoach South Ltd, 112 Malling Street, Lewes, East Sussex, BN7 2RB

The Stagecoach South group now covers much of the southern coast, and was restructured from 29th March 1992 into three divisions to cover operations at that time: Stagecoach South Ltd, Sussex Coastline Buses Ltd and South Coast Buses Ltd. These covered the former operations of the Southdown empire, Hampshire Bus and the former Hastings operations of Maidstone & District. To these was added Stagecoach Hants & Surrey when Alder Valley was purchased in October 1992, and Stagecoach East Kent upon the absorption of the East Kent Travel group in September 1993.

The individual identity of the constituent companies, particularly the more recent, can still be detected, though Stagecoach livery has now obliterated the former Southdown colours and is prevalent in the former Alder Valley area. East Kent colours of burgundy and cream, with a yellow-based scheme relieved by red and black for minibuses, is still predominant at the east of the area. Stagecoach influence is increasingly evident with the arrival of new vehicles from group orders. A certain amount of interchange with other Stagecoach fleets has also occurred to promote the withdrawal of older or non-standard types.

Stagecoach South Ltd trades as Hampshire Bus with depots at Andover, Basingstoke and Winchester and outstations at Alton, Bishops Waltham, Marlborough, Petersfield and Stockbridge. South Coast Buses Ltd has depots at Eastbourne and Hastings with outstations at Lewes, Rye, Seaford and Uckfield. Sussex Coastline has depots at Chichester, Havant and Worthing, with outstations at Henfield and Littlehampton. Stagecoach Hants & Surrey is based at Aldershot and Hindhead with an outstation at Alton. Stagecoach East Kent operates at Ashford, Dover, Folkestone, Herne Bay and Thanet (Ramsgate) with outstations at Canterbury, Deal and New Romney.

One of the huge armada of Bristol VRTs with Eastern Coach Works bodies inherited from Southdown, No.367 is less usual in carrying dual-purpose seating; its original Leyland engine has also been superseded by standard Gardner 6LXB units. This view was taken at Portsmouth Hard on 5th June 1994. Calvin Churchill

So far none of the home-grown minibuses of East Kent have succumbed to Stagecoach colours, remaining in their colourful Minilink garb. No.47, an Iveco with Carlyle bodywork, was on layover at Pencester Road, Dover on 24th March 1994 outside the newly-built travel office. Paul Gainsbury

A quantity of Volvo B10Ms with Alexander bodywork from the 1994 Stagecoach group order has been sent to Stagecoach South, finding a variety of uses. No.621 passes through Worthing in June 1994 on the limited stop service to Brighton, still devoid of fleet identity after entering service. Calvin Churchill

East Kent completed their one-man conversion programme with standard Bristol VRT/Eastern Coach Works double-deckers in the early 1980s. No.7669 waits to cross onto the main road at Nickle bend whilst working a school service on 10th September 1993. Nicholas King

East Kent's Leyland Olympians with Northern Counties bodywork, all new in the past four years, have received Stagecoach livery quicker than other types. No.7813 takes layover at Canterbury Bus Station on 24th March 1994 before returning to its home at Folkestone. Paul Gainsbury

Olympians of the early 1990s included several on lengthened chassis with coach-seated bodywork by Alexander. No.221, passes through Sussex scenery on 19th March 1994, showing the frontal upper-deck stripes which are now being discontinued from the livery. Calvin Churchill

Amongst a horde of Leyland Nationals acquired with Alder Valley in the autumn of 1992, No.1247 dates from 1976. By the time this shot was taken in Winchester on 1st October 1993 it had received Stagecoach livery with Hampshire Bus names. Calvin Churchill

A major order fulfilled during 1992 for Stagecoach South comprised 80 Dennis Darts with Alexander bodywork. No.553 arrives at West Street, Chichester on 24th November 1992 soon after being delivered to the Sussex Coastline fleet. Later arrivals were to be diverted to enable upgrading of the recently-acquired Alder Valley sector. Nicholas King

The last AEC Regent V in service with an established operator in the area, No.0946 was one of East Kent's last order received in 1967 with Park Royal bodywork. After a considerable period as a mobile office it was returned to public service at Hastings and was photographed at Malvern Way working a peak-hour journey to cope with summer student traffic. Terry Blackman

Amongst the other special events vehicles retained by Stagecoach South have been two of the renowned 'Queen Mary' class of Leyland PD3/4s with Northern Counties convertible bodies from 1964. No.0409 works the summer service from Lewes to the Bluebell Railway. Malcolm King

Two Leyland Swifts with Wadham Stringer bodywork are on extended loan from East Sussex County Council for use on County Rider services. G92VMM, technically numbered 2892, threads its way through the narrow streets of Newhaven in February 1994. Terry Blackman

Seen at Basingstoke bus station with the Hampshire Travel coach unit of Stagecoach South, No.1006 is a Plaxton Paramount bodied Volvo B10M formerly with Hampshire Bus. Colin Lloyd

Acquired with the Alder Valley fleet, No.494 is an Iveco Daily with Carlyle bodywork new in 1989. It was photographed in Aldershot in June 1993. Calvin Churchill

The Stagecoach group lost little time in reducing the surviving older minibuses of East Kent, injecting eight Ivecos from the East Midland fleet. No.467, with Robin Hood bodywork, passes the bus station at Canterbury in March 1994. Calvin Churchill

STAGECOACH SOUTH

1	H101EKR	Iveco Daily 49.10	Phoenix	B23F	1991	
2	H102EKR	Iveco Daily 49.10	Phoenix	B23F	1991	
3	H103EKR	Iveco Daily 49.10	Phoenix	B23F	1991	
4	H104EKR	Iveco Daily 49.10	Phoenix	B23F	1991	
5	D935EBP	Iveco Daily 49.10	Robin Hood City Nippy	B19F	1987	
6	D226VCD	Iveco Daily 49.10	Robin Hood City Nippy	B21F	1986	Ex Brighton & Hove, 1990
10	D230VCD	Iveco Daily 49.10	Robin Hood City Nippy	B21F	1986	Ex Brighton & Hove, 1990
11	J121LKO	Iveco Daily 49.10	Dormobile Routemaker	B23F	1991	
12	J112LKO	Iveco Daily 49.10	Carlyle Dailybus	B23F	1991	
13	J113LKO	Iveco Daily 49.10	Carlyle Dailybus	B23F	1991	
14	J114LKO	Iveco Daily 49.10	Carlyle Dailybus	B23F	1991	

15-20   Iveco Daily 49.10   Dormobile Routemaker   B23F   1991

15	J115LKO	17	J117LKO	19	J119LKO
16	J116LKO	18	J118LKO	20	J120LKO

21-26   Iveco Daily 49.10   Robin Hood City Nippy   B23F   1989   Ex Magicbus, Perth, 1990

21	F21PSL	22	F22PSL	23	F23PSL	25	F25PSL	26	F26PSL

30	G30PSR	Iveco Daily 49.10	Phoenix (1990)	B23F	1989	Ex Magicbus, Perth, 1990
31	F61AVV	Iveco Daily 49.10	Robin Hood City Nippy	B25F	1989	
32	F62AVV	Iveco Daily 49.10	Robin Hood City Nippy	B25F	1989	
33	E233JRF	Iveco Daily 49.10	Robin Hood City Nippy	DP25F	1987	Ex Chatfield, Worthing, 1989
34	G34PSR	Iveco Daily 49.10	Robin Hood City Nippy	B23F	1989	Ex Magicbus, Perth, 1990
35	G35PSR	Iveco Daily 49.10	Robin Hood City Nippy	B23F	1989	Ex East Midland, 1993
36	G36SSR	Iveco Daily 49.10	Phoenix	B23F	1989	Ex Magicbus, Perth, 1990
37	G37SSR	Iveco Daily 49.10	Phoenix	B23F	1989	Ex Magicbus, Perth, 1990
38	G38SSR	Iveco Daily 49.10	Phoenix	B23F	1989	Ex Magicbus, Perth, 1990
39	G39SSR	Iveco Daily 49.10	Phoenix	B23F	1989	Ex Magicbus, Perth, 1990
41	D231VCD	Iveco Daily 49.10	Robin Hood City Nippy	B21F	1986	Ex Brighton & Hove, 1990
42	G42SSR	Iveco Daily 49.10	Phoenix	B23F	1989	Ex Magicbus, Perth, 1990
43	G43SSR	Iveco Daily 49.10	Phoenix	B23F	1989	Ex Magicbus, Perth, 1990
45	E65BVS	Iveco Daily 49.10	Robin Hood City Nippy	B25F	1988	Ex Chatfield, Worthing, 1989
46	G446VKK	Iveco Daily 49.10	Carlyle Dailybus	B23F	1990	
47	G447VKK	Iveco Daily 49.10	Carlyle Dailybus	B23F	1990	

51-70   Iveco Daily 49.10   Robin Hood City Nippy   B23F   1987

51	E151UKR	55	E155UKR	59	E159UKR	63	E163UKR	67	E167UKR
52	E152UKR	56	E156UKR	60	E160UKR	64	E164UKR	68	E168UKR
53	E153UKR	57	E157UKR	61	E161UKR	65	E165UKR	69	E169UKR
54	E154UKR	58	E158UKR	62	E162UKR	66	E166UKR	70	E170UKR

71-75   Iveco Daily 49.10   Robin Hood City Nippy   B23F   1989

71	F71FKK	72	F72FKK	73	F73FKK	74	F74FKK	75	F75FKK

80-87   Iveco Daily 49.10   Robin Hood City Nippy   B19F   1987

80	E580TKJ	82	E582TKJ	84	E584TKJ	86	E586TKJ
81	E581TKJ	83	E583TKJ	85	E585TKJ	87	E587TKJ

91	G491RKK	Iveco Daily 49.10	Carlyle Dailybus	B23F	1990
92	G492RKK	Iveco Daily 49.10	Carlyle Dailybus	B23F	1990
93	G493RKK	Iveco Daily 49.10	Carlyle Dailybus	B23F	1990
94	G494RKK	Iveco Daily 49.10	Carlyle Dailybus	B23F	1990
95	G95SKR	Iveco Daily 49.10	Phoenix	B23F	1990
96	G96SKR	Iveco Daily 49.10	Phoenix	B23F	1990
97	G97SKR	Iveco Daily 49.10	Phoenix	B23F	1990
98	G98SKR	Iveco Daily 49.10	Phoenix	B23F	1990

100-105   Leyland National 11351A/1R   B52F   1979

100	AYJ100T	102	AYJ102T	104	AYJ104T
101	AYJ101T	103	AYJ103T	105	AYJ105T

| 106 | DRU6T | Leyland National 11351A/1R | | | | | | | B49F | 1979 | |

107-118 Leyland National 11351A/1R B52F 1979

107	AYJ107T	111	ENJ911V	114	ENJ914V	117	ENJ917V
109	ENJ909V	112	ENJ912V	115	ENJ915V	118	ENJ918V
110	ENJ910V	113	ENJ913V	116	ENJ916V		

119-126 Leyland National 2 NL116L11/1R B52F 1980

| 119 | GYG919V | 121 | GYG921V | 123 | HFG923V | 125 | OUF262W |
| 120 | GYG920V | 122 | GYG922V | 124 | JNJ194V | 126 | SYC852 |

| 127 | FDV830V | Leyland National 2 NL116L11/1R | B52F | 1980 | Ex Devon General, 1989 |
| 128 | FDV831V | Leyland National 2 NL116L11/1R | B52F | 1980 | Ex Devon General, 1989 |

129-138 Leyland National 2 NL116AL11/1R B49F 1981

| 129 | 415DCD | 131 | 411DCD | 133 | 420DCD | 135 | 405DCD | 137 | 407DCD |
| 130 | 400DCD | 132 | YLJ332 | 134 | HUF451X | 136 | 406DCD | 138 | 410DCD |

139	FDV829V	Leyland National 2 NL116L11/1R	B52F	1980	Ex Devon General, 1989
140	CPO98W	Leyland National 2 NL106L11/1R	B41F	1980	Ex Portsmouth, 1990
141	CPO99W	Leyland National 2 NL106L11/1R	DP40F	1980	Ex Portsmouth, 1990
142	CPO100W	Leyland National 2 NL106L11/1R	DP40F	1980	Ex Portsmouth, 1990
143	ERV115W	Leyland National 2 NL106AL11/1R	B41F	1981	Ex Portsmouth, 1990
144	ERV116W	Leyland National 2 NL106AL11/1R	B41F	1981	Ex Portsmouth, 1990
145	ERV117W	Leyland National 2 NL106AL11/1R	B41F	1981	Ex Portsmouth, 1990
146	ERV118W	Leyland National 2 NL106AL11/1R	B41F	1981	Ex Portsmouth, 1990
148	UFG48S	Leyland National 11351A/2R	B52F	1977	
151	WPR151S	Leyland National 11351A/1R	B49F	1978	
152	WPR152S	Leyland National 11351A/1R	B49F	1977	
153	VOD603S	Leyland National 11351A/1R	B52F	1978	Ex Devon General, 1987
154	VOD604S	Leyland National 11351A/1R	B52F	1978	Ex Devon General, 1987
155	VOD605S	Leyland National 11351A/1R	B52F	1978	Ex Devon General, 1987
156	WFX256S	Leyland National 11351A/1R	DP48F	1978	
157	UHG757R	Leyland National 11351A/1R	B52F	1977	Ex Ribble, 1993
161	TRN811V	Leyland National 10351B/1R	B44F	1979	Ex Magicbus, Perth, 1991
162	FPR62V	Leyland National 11351A/1R	B49F	1979	
163	PCD73R	Leyland National 11351A/1R	B49F	1976	
164	VFX984S	Leyland National 11351A/1R	B49F	1978	
165	VOD625S	Leyland National 11351A/1R	B52F	1978	Ex Devon General, 1987
166	MLJ922P	Leyland National 11351/1R	B49F	1976	
168	WYJ168S	Leyland National 11351A/2R	B48F	1978	
169	WYJ169S	Leyland National 11351A/2R	B48F	1978	
170	TEL490R	Leyland National 11351A/1R	DP48F	1977	
171	WYJ171S	Leyland National 11351A/2R	B44D	1978	
172	PCD82R	Leyland National 11351A/1R	B49F	1977	
173	YCD73T	Leyland National 11351A/2R	B52F	1978	
174	YCD74T	Leyland National 11351A/2R	B48F	1978	
176	YCD76T	Leyland National 11351A/2R	B48F	1978	
177	YCD77T	Leyland National 11351A/2R	B48F	1978	
178	PCD78R	Leyland National 11351A/1R	B49F	1976	
179	PCD79R	Leyland National 11351A/1R	B49F	1977	
180	PCD80R	Leyland National 11351A/1R	B49F	1977	
182	YCD82T	Leyland National 11351A/2R	B48F	1978	
183	UFX853S	Leyland National 11351A/1R	B49F	1977	
187	YCD87T	Leyland National 11351A/2R	B48F	1978	
188	CBV798S	Leyland National 11351A/1R	B49F	1978	Ex Ribble, 1986

189-195 Leyland National 11351A/1R B52F 1979

| 189 | AYJ89T | 192 | AYJ92T | 194 | AYJ94T |
| 191 | AYJ91T | 193 | AYJ93T | 195 | AYJ95T |

196	RJT146R	Leyland National 11351A/1R	B49F	1977
197	AYJ97T	Leyland National 11351A/1R	B52F	1979
198	AYJ98T	Leyland National 11351A/1R	B52F	1979

201-206   Leyland Olympian ON2R56G13Z4   Alexander RL   H51/36F   1988

201	F601MSL	203	F603MSL	205	F605MSL
202	F602MSL	204	F604MSL	206	F606MSL

207-214   Leyland Olympian ON2R56G13Z4   Alexander RL   DPH51/31F   1989

207	G807RTS	209	G809RTS	211	G211SSL	213	G213SSL
208	G808RTS	210	G210SSL	212	G212SSL	214	G214SSL

215-219   Leyland Olympian ON2R56G13Z4   Alexander RL   H51/34F   1990

215	H815CBP	216	H816CBP	217	H817CBP	218	H818CBP	219	H819CBP

220	J720GAP	Leyland Olympian ON2R56G13Z4 Alexander RL	DPH47/27F	1991
221	J721GAP	Leyland Olympian ON2R56G13Z4 Alexander RL	DPH47/27F	1991
222	J722GAP	Leyland Olympian ON2R56G13Z4 Alexander RL	DPH47/27F	1991
223	J623GCR	Leyland Olympian ON2R56G13Z4 Alexander RL	H47/30F	1991
224	J624GCR	Leyland Olympian ON2R56G13Z4 Alexander RL	H47/30F	1991

225-234   Leyland Olympian ON2R56G13Z4   Alexander RL   H51/34F   1990

225	G705TCD	227	G707TCD	229	G709TCD	231	G701TCD	233	G703TCD
226	G706TCD	228	G708TCD	230	G710TCD	232	G702TCD	234	G704TCD

235-240   Leyland Olympian ON2R50G13Z4   Alexander RL   DPH43/27F   1992

235	K235NHC	237	K237NHC	239	K239NHC
236	K236NHC	238	K238NHC	240	K240NHC

241-250   Volvo Olympian YN2RV18Z4   Northern Counties Countybus Palatine   DPH43/25F   1993

241	L241SDY	243	L243SDY	245	L245SDY	247	L247SDY	249	L249SDY
242	L242SDY	244	L244SDY	246	L246SDY	248	L248SDY	250	L250SDY

301-309   Volvo Citybus D10M-50   Northern Counties   DPH43/33F   1989

301	F301MYJ	303	F303MYJ	305	F305MYJ	307	F307MYJ	309	F309MYJ
302	F302MYJ	304	F304MYJ	306	F306MYJ	308	F308MYJ		

315	GLJ467N	Bristol VRT/SL2/6LX	Eastern Coach Works	H43/31F	1974	
321	VTV171S	Bristol VRT/SL3/6LXB	Eastern Coach Works	H43/31F	1978	Ex East Midland, 1993
322	VTV172S	Bristol VRT/SL3/6LXB	Eastern Coach Works	H43/31F	1978	Ex East Midland, 1993
323	XRR173S	Bristol VRT/SL3/6LXB	Eastern Coach Works	H43/31F	1978	Ex East Midland, 1993
324	XAP644S	Bristol VRT/SL3/6LXB	Eastern Coach Works	H43/31F	1978	
336	XAP636S	Bristol VRT/SL3/6LXB	Eastern Coach Works	H43/31F	1978	
347	AAP647T	Bristol VRT/SL3/6LXB	Eastern Coach Works	H43/31F	1978	
348	AAP648T	Bristol VRT/SL3/6LXB	Eastern Coach Works	H43/31F	1978	

351-358   Bristol VRT/SL3/6LXB   Eastern Coach Works   H43/31F   1980

351	JWV251W	353	JWV253W	356	JWV256W
352	JWV252W	355	JWV255W	358	JWV258W

359	DBV29W	Bristol VRT/SL3/6LXB	Eastern Coach Works	DPH43/31F	1980	Ex Ribble, 1986
365	DBV25W	Bristol VRT/SL3/6LXB	Eastern Coach Works	DPH43/31F	1980	Ex Ribble, 1986
366	JWV266W	Bristol VRT/SL3/680	Eastern Coach Works	H43/31F	1981	now Gardner 6LXB engine
367	JWV267W	Bristol VRT/SL3/680	Eastern Coach Works	DPH43/27F	1981	now Gardner 6LXB engine
368	JWV268W	Bristol VRT/SL3/680	Eastern Coach Works	H43/31F	1981	now Gardner 6LXB engine
369	JWV269W	Bristol VRT/SL3/680	Eastern Coach Works	H43/31F	1981	now Gardner 6LXB engine
372	AAP672T	Bristol VRT/SL3/6LXB	Eastern Coach Works	H43/28F	1979	
374	JWV274W	Bristol VRT/SL3/680	Eastern Coach Works	H43/31F	1981	
375	JWV275W	Bristol VRT/SL3/680	Eastern Coach Works	H43/31F	1981	
376	JWV976W	Bristol VRT/SL3/680	Eastern Coach Works	H43/31F	1981	now Gardner 6LXB engine
377	EAP977V	Bristol VRT/SL3/6LXB	Eastern Coach Works	H43/31F	1979	
380	EAP980V	Bristol VRT/SL3/6LXB	Eastern Coach Works	H43/31F	1979	
382	EAP982V	Bristol VRT/SL3/6LXB	Eastern Coach Works	H43/31F	1979	

387-396   Bristol VRT/SL3/6LXB   Eastern Coach Works   H43/31F   1978

| 387 | VPR486S | 392 | VPR491S | 394 | HFG193T | 396 | YEL3T |
| 391 | VPR490S | 393 | VPR492S | 395 | YEL2T | | |

422-450   Bristol VRT/SL3/6LXB   Eastern Coach Works   H43/31F   1979-80 Ex Devon General, 1988-89

422	FDV818V	435	FDV839V	440	KRU840W	446	LFJ874W	449	LFJ875W
432	ELJ212V	438	KRU838W	441	KRU841W	448	LFJ881W	450	LFJ880W
433	FDV834V	439	KRU839W	444	KRU844W	448	LFJ870W		

460-467   Iveco Daily 49.10   Robin Hood City Nippy   B25F   1989   Ex East Midland, 1993

| 460 | G910KWF | 461 | G911KWF | 463 | G913KWF | 464 | G914KWF | 467 | G917KWF |

469-476   Iveco Daily 49.10   Robin Hood City Nippy   B21F   1986

| 469 | D469WPM | 470 | D470WPM | 471 | D471WPM | 473 | D473WPM | 476 | D476WPM |

477	E201EPB	Iveco Daily 49.10	Robin Hood City Nippy	B25F	1987	
478	E202EPB	Iveco Daily 49.10	Robin Hood City Nippy	B25F	1987	
479	E203EPB	Iveco Daily 49.10	Robin Hood City Nippy	B25F	1987	
480	E204EPB	Iveco Daily 49.10	Robin Hood City Nippy	B25F	1987	
481	G921KWF	Iveco Daily 49.10	Robin Hood City Nippy	B23F	1989	Ex East Midland, 1993
482	G922KWF	Iveco Daily 49.10	Robin Hood City Nippy	B25F	1990	Ex East Midland, 1993
483	G923KWF	Iveco Daily 49.10	Robin Hood City Nippy	B25F	1990	Ex East Midland, 1993
485	F695OPA	Iveco Daily 49.10	Carlyle Dailybus	B23F	1988	

488-492   Iveco Daily 49.10   Phoenix   B23F   1989

| 488 | G418RYJ | 489 | G419RYJ | 490 | G420RYJ | 491 | G421RYJ | 492 | G422RYJ |

| 494 | G864BPD | Iveco Daily 49.10 | Carlyle Dailybus | B23F | 1989 | |
| 497 | J416TGM | Iveco Daily 49.10 | Reeve Burgess | B25F | 1991 | |

501-580   Dennis Dart 9.8SDL3017   Alexander Dash   B40F*   1992   * 501-34 are B41F

501	J501GCD	517	J517GCD	533	J533GCD	549	J549GCD	565	K565NHC
502	J502GCD	518	J518GCD	534	J534GCD	550	J550GCD	566	K566NHC
503	J503GCD	519	J519GCD	535	J535GCD	551	J551GCD	567	K567NHC
504	J504GCD	520	J520GCD	536	J536GCD	552	J552GCD	568	K568NHC
505	J505GCD	521	J521GCD	537	J537GCD	553	K553NHC	569	K569NHC
506	J506GCD	522	J522GCD	538	J538GCD	554	K554NHC	570	K570NHC
507	J507GCD	523	J523GCD	539	J539GCD	555	K655NHC	571	K571NHC
508	J508GCD	524	J524GCD	540	J540GCD	556	K556NHC	572	K572NHC
509	J509GCD	525	J525GCD	541	J541GCD	557	K557NHC	573	K573NHC
510	J510GCD	526	J526GCD	542	J542GCD	558	K558NHC	574	K574NHC
511	J511GCD	527	J527GCD	543	J543GCD	559	K559NHC	574	K575NHC
512	J512GCD	528	J528GCD	544	J544GCD	560	K660NHC	576	K576NHC
513	J513GCD	529	J529GCD	545	J545GCD	561	K561NHC	577	K577NHC
514	J514GCD	530	J530GCD	546	J546GCD	562	K562NHC	578	K578NHC
515	J515GCD	531	J531GCD	547	J547GCD	563	K563NHC	579	K579NHC
516	J516GCD	532	J532GCD	548	J548GCD	564	K564NHC	580	K580NHC

581	J701YRM	Dennis Dart 9.8SDL3017	Alexander Dash	B40F	1991	Ex Cumberland, 1992
582	J702YRM	Dennis Dart 9.8SDL3017	Alexander Dash	B41F	1991	Ex Cumberland, 1992
583	J703YRM	Dennis Dart 9.8SDL3017	Alexander Dash	B41F	1992	Ex Cumberland, 1992

584-588   Dennis Dart 9.8SDL3017   Alexander Dash   B40F*   1992   * 584 is B41F

| 584 | K584ODY | 585 | K585ODY | 586 | K586ODY | 587 | K587ODY | 588 | K588ODY |

589	K789DAO	Volvo B10M-55	Alexander PS	DP48F	1993	Ex Cumberland, 1994
590	K790DAO	Volvo B10M-55	Alexander PS	DP48F	1993	Ex Cumberland, 1994
591	K791DAO	Volvo B10M-55	Alexander PS	DP48F	1993	Ex Cumberland, 1994

596-600   Volvo B10M-55   Alexander PS   DP48F   1994

| 596 | L346KCK | 597 | L347KCK | 598 | L338KCK | 599 | | 600 | |

601-605 — Volvo B10M-55 — Northern Counties Countybus Paladin — DP49F — 1994

601 L601VCD	**602** L602VCD	**603** L603VCD	**604** L604VCD	**605** L605VCD

606-635 — Volvo B10M-55 — Alexander PS — DP48F — 1994

606 L606TDY	**612** M612APN	**618** L618TDY	**624** L624TDY	**630** L630TDY
607 L607TDY	**613** M613APN	**619** L619TDY	**625** L625TDY	**631** L631TDY
608 L608TDY	**614** M614APN	**620** L620TDY	**626** L626TDY	**632** L632TDY
609 L609TDY	**615** M615APN	**621** L621TDY	**627** L627TDY	**633** L633TDY
610 M610APN	**616** L616TDY	**622** L622TDY	**628** L628TDY	**634** L634TDY
611 M611APN	**617** L617TDY	**623** L623TDY	**629** L629TDY	**635** L635TDY

657 LHG437T	Bristol VRT/SL3/501	Eastern Coach Works	H43/31F	1978	Ex Ribble, 1986
658 LHG438T	Bristol VRT/SL3/501	Eastern Coach Works	H43/31F	1978	Ex Ribble, 1986

660-671 — Bristol VRT/SL3/6LXB — Eastern Coach Works — H43/28F — 1978-79

660 AAP660T	**668** AAP668T	**670** AAP670T	**671** AAP671T	**672** AAP672T

673-692 — Bristol VRT/SL3/6LXB — Eastern Coach Works — H43/31F — 1979-80

673 EAP973V	**684** EAP984V	**687** EAP987V	**691** EAP991V
678 EAP978V	**685** EAP985V	**688** EAP988V	**692** EAP992V
683 EAP983V	**686** EAP986V	**690** EAP990V	

693 ELJ213V	Bristol VRT/SL3/6LXB	Eastern Coach Works	H43/31F	1979
696 EAP996V	Bristol VRT/SL3/6LXB	Eastern Coach Works	H43/31F	1980
729 WKO129S	Bristol VRT/SL3/6LXB	Eastern Coach Works	H43/31F	1978 Ex Maidstone & District, 1983

749-760 — Bristol VRT/SL3/6LXB — Eastern Coach Works — H43/31F — 1979 Ex Maidstone & District, 1983

749 BKE849T	**751** BKE851T	**759** BKE859T
750 BKE850T	**758** BKE858T	**760** BKE860T

761 RJT151R	Bristol VRT/SL3/6LXB	Eastern Coach Works	H43/31F	1977
762 BKE862T	Bristol VRT/SL3/6LXB	Eastern Coach Works	H43/31F	1979 Ex Maidstone & District, 1983
780 BAU180T	Bristol VRT/SL3/6LXB	Eastern Coach Works	H43/31F	1978 Ex East Midland, 1993
782 AET182T	Bristol VRT/SL3/6LXB	Eastern Coach Works	H43/31F	1979 Ex East Midland, 1993
786 AET186T	Bristol VRT/SL3/6LXB	Eastern Coach Works	H43/31F	1979 Ex East Midland, 1993
787 AET187T	Bristol VRT/SL3/6LXB	Eastern Coach Works	H43/31F	1979 Ex East Midland, 1993
800 C800SDY	Mercedes-Benz L608D	Alexander AM	B20F	1986
828 D228UHC	Mercedes-Benz L608D	Alexander AM	B20F	1986
830 D230UHC	Mercedes-Benz L608D	Alexander AM	B20F	1986

841-850 — Mercedes-Benz 709D — Alexander AM — B23F* — 1990 — * 841-3 are B25F

841 G71APO	**843** G73APO	**845** G975ARV	**847** G977ARV	**849** G979ARV
842 G72APO	**844** G974ARV	**846** G976ARV	**848** G978ARV	**850** G980ARV

853-888 — Mercedes-Benz 709D — Alexander(Belfast) — B25F — 1993

853 K853ODY	**861** K861ODY	**869** K869ODY	**877** K877ODY	**885** L885SDY
854 K854ODY	**862** K862ODY	**870** K870ODY	**878** K878ODY	**886** L886SDY
855 K855ODY	**863** K863ODY	**871** K871ODY	**879** K879ODY	**887** L887SDY
856 K856ODY	**864** K864ODY	**872** K872ODY	**880** K880ODY	**888** L188SDY
857 K857ODY	**865** K865ODY	**873** K873ODY	**881** L881SDY	
858 K858ODY	**866** K866ODY	**874** K874ODY	**882** L882SDY	
859 K859ODY	**867** K867ODY	**875** K875ODY	**883** L883SDY	
860 K860ODY	**868** K868ODY	**876** K876ODY	**884** L884SDY	

950-980 — Bristol VRT/SL3/6LXB — Eastern Coach Works — H43/31F — 1978-80 Ex Thames Valley & Aldershot, 1986

950 TPE156S	**961** GGM81W	**967** WJM827T	**979** CJH119V	**995** GGM105W
953 VPF283S	**962** GGM82W	**968** WJM828T	**980** CJH120V	
955 GGM85W	**964** WJM824T	**969** WJM829T	**982** CJH142V	
956 GGM86W	**965** WJM825T	**972** WJM832T	**985** CJH145V	
960 GGM80W	**966** WJM826T	**977** CJH117V	**988** KKK888V	

1001	401DCD	Leyland Tiger TRCTL11/2R	Plaxton Paramount 3200	C50F	1983	
1002	402DCD	Leyland Tiger TRCTL11/2R	Plaxton Paramount 3200	C50F	1983	
1003	403DCD	Leyland Tiger TRCTL11/3R	Plaxton Paramount 3200	C50F	1983	
1004	BYJ919Y	Leyland Tiger TRCTL11/3R	Plaxton Paramount 3200	C50F	1983	
1005	UWP105	Leyland Tiger TRCTL11/3R	Plaxton Paramount 3200	C50F	1983	
1006	896HOD	Volvo B10M-61	Plaxton Paramount 3500 2	C40FT	1985	Ex Fife Scottish, 1991
1007	495FFJ	Volvo B10M-61	Plaxton Paramount 3500 2	C52F	1985	Ex Fife Scottish, 1991
1008	408DCD	Leyland Leopard PSU5D/4R	Plaxton Paramount 3200(1984)	C53F	1981	
1012	412DCD	Leyland Leopard PSU5E/4R	Plaxton Supreme V	C50F	1982	
1013	413DCD	Leyland Leopard PSU5E/4R	Plaxton Supreme V	C50F	1982	
1017	NFX667	Leyland Leopard PSU5E/4R	Plaxton Supreme V	C50F	1982	
1064	VSV564	Leyland Tiger TRCTL11/3R	Plaxton Paramount 3200Exp	C49F	1983	Ex Maidstone & District, 1985
1066	MSU466	Leyland Tiger TRCTL11/3RH	Duple 340	C53FT	1987	Ex Fife Scottish, 1991
1072	USV672	Leyland Tiger TRCTL11/3R	Plaxton Paramount 3200Exp	C49F	1983	Ex Maidstone & District, 1985
1084	C84PRP	Leyland Tiger TRCTL11/3RZ	Plaxton Paramount 3500 2	C46FT	1986	Ex United Counties, 1993
1094	GPJ894N	Leyland National 11351/1R		B49F	1975	Ex The Bee Line, 1992
1115	MFN115R	Leyland National 11351A/1R		B49F	1976	
1118	MFN118R	Leyland National 11351A/1R		B49F	1976	
1170	ELJ208V	Leyland Leopard PSU3E/4R	Plaxton Supreme IV Exp	C53F	1979	Ex Shamrock & Rambler, 1984
1176	NPJ476R	Leyland National 11351A/1R		B49F	1976	Ex Thames Valley & Aldershot, 1986
1180	UMO180N	Leyland National 11351/1R		B49F	1974	

1181-1189 Leyland National 11351A/1R — DP48F 1977

1181	NFN81R	**1184**	NFN84R	**1187**	NFN87R	**1189** NFN89R
1183	NFN83R	**1186**	NFN86R	**1188**	NFN88R	

1193	YEL93Y	Leyland Leopard PSU5E/4R	Eastern Coach Works B51	C52F	1982	Ex Pilgrim Coaches, 1987
1194	YEL94Y	Leyland Leopard PSU5E/4R	Eastern Coach Works B51	C52F	1982	Ex Pilgrim Coaches, 1987
1201	HPK503N	Leyland National 11351/1R		B49F	1975	Ex Thames Valley & Aldershot, 1986
1203	HPK505N	Leyland National 11351/1R		B49F	1975	Ex Thames Valley & Aldershot, 1986
1214	KPA365P	Leyland National 11351/1R		B49F	1975	Ex Thames Valley & Aldershot, 1986
1215	KPA366P	Leyland National 11351/1R		B49F	1975	Ex Thames Valley & Aldershot, 1986
1217	KPA368P	Leyland National 11351/1R		B49F	1975	Ex Thames Valley & Aldershot, 1986
1218	KPA369P	Leyland National 11351/1R		B49F	1975	Ex Thames Valley & Aldershot, 1986
1223	KPA374P	Leyland National 11351/1R		B49F	1975	Ex Thames Valley & Aldershot, 1986
1227	KPA378P	Leyland National 11351/1R		B49F	1975	Ex Thames Valley & Aldershot, 1986
1228	KPA379P	Leyland National 11351/1R		B49F	1975	Ex Thames Valley & Aldershot, 1986
1232	KPA383P	Leyland National 11351/1R		B49F	1975	Ex Thames Valley & Aldershot, 1986
1236	KPA387P	Leyland National 11351A/1R		B49F	1976	Ex Thames Valley & Aldershot, 1986
1237	KPA388P	Leyland National 11351A/1R		B49F	1976	Ex Thames Valley & Aldershot, 1986
1238	KPA389P	Leyland National 11351A/1R		B49F	1976	Ex Thames Valley & Aldershot, 1986
1247	LPF605P	Leyland National 11351/1R/SC		B49F	1976	Ex Thames Valley & Aldershot, 1986
1253	NPJ474R	Leyland National 11351A/1R		B49F	1976	Ex Thames Valley & Aldershot, 1986
1256	NPJ477R	Leyland National 11351A/1R		B49F	1976	Ex Thames Valley & Aldershot, 1986
1259	NPJ480R	Leyland National 11351A/1R		B49F	1976	Ex Thames Valley & Aldershot, 1986
1261	NPJ482R	Leyland National 11351A/1R		B49F	1976	Ex Thames Valley & Aldershot, 1986
1264	NPJ485R	Leyland National 11351A/1R		B49F	1977	Ex Thames Valley & Aldershot, 1986
1271	TPE148S	Leyland National 11351A/1R		B49F	1977	Ex Thames Valley & Aldershot, 1986
1272	TPE149S	Leyland National 11351A/1R		B49F	1977	Ex Thames Valley & Aldershot, 1986
1273	TPE150S	Leyland National 11351A/1R		B49F	1977	Ex Thames Valley & Aldershot, 1986
1276	TPE169S	Leyland National 11351A/1R		DP45F	1978	Ex Thames Valley & Aldershot, 1986
1279	VPF295S	Leyland National 11351A/1R		DP45F	1978	Ex Thames Valley & Aldershot, 1986
1344	PJJ344S	Leyland National 10351A/1R		B41F	1977	
1345	PJJ345S	Leyland National 10351A/1R		B41F	1977	
1346	PJJ346S	Leyland National 10351A/1R		B41F	1977	
1401	J401LKO	DAF SB220LC550	Optare Delta	B49F	1991	
1402	J402LKO	DAF SB220LC550	Optare Delta	B49F	1991	
1403	J403LKO	DAF SB220LC550	Optare Delta	B49F	1991	
1546	GFN546N	Leyland National 10351/1R		B40F	1975	
1552	GFN552N	Leyland National 10351/1R		B37F	1975	

1890-1900 Leyland National 11351A/1R — B49F 1976

1890	JJG890P	**1893**	JJG893P	**1898**	JJG898P	
1892	JJG892P	**1895**	JJG895P	**1900**	JJG900P	

2712	C712FKE	Ford Transit 190L	Dormobile	B16F	1986	
2742	C742HKK	Freight Rover Sherpa 365	Dormobile	B16F	1986	

94

2891	G91VMM	Leyland Swift LBM6T/2RA	Wadham Stringer Vanguard	B34FL	1990	On extended hire from East Sussex County Council
2892	G92VMM	Leyland Swift LBM6T/2RA	Wadham Stringer Vanguard	B34FL	1990	On extended hire from East Sussex County Council
2901	F561HPP	MCW Metrorider MF158/9	MCW	B33F	1988	Ex Chatfield, Worthing, 1989
2902	F562HPP	MCW Metrorider MF158/9	MCW	B33F	1988	Ex Chatfield, Worthing, 1989
2903	F563HPP	MCW Metrorider MF158/9	MCW	B33F	1988	Ex Chatfield, Worthing, 1989
2904	F564HPP	MCW Metrorider MF158/9	MCW	B33F	1988	Ex Chatfield, Worthing, 1989
2906	416DCD	MCW Metrorider MF158/10	MCW	B31F	1988	Ex East Midland, 1989
2907	417DCD	MCW Metrorider MF154/1	MCW	B31F	1988	Ex East Midland, 1989
2908	418DCD	MCW Metrorider MF158/3	MCW	DP33F	1988	Ex East Midland, 1989
2909	419DCD	MCW Metrorider MF158/9	MCW	DP28F	1988	Ex Chatfield, Worthing, 1989

7016-7024   Bristol VRT/SL3/6LXB   Willowbrook   H43/31F   1977-78

7016	PJJ16S	7021	PJJ21S	7022	PJJ22S	7023	PJJ23S	7024	PJJ24S

7043	MFN43R	Bristol VRT/SL3/6LXB	Eastern Coach Works	H43/31F	1976	
7046	MFN46R	Bristol VRT/SL3/6LXB	Eastern Coach Works	H43/31F	1976	
7611	UWV611S	Bristol VRT/SL3/6LXB	Eastern Coach Works	CO43/31F	1978	
7613	UWV613S	Bristol VRT/SL3/6LXB	Eastern Coach Works	CO43/31F	1977	Ex Southdown, 1991
7614	UWV614S	Bristol VRT/SL3/6LXB	Eastern Coach Works	CO43/31F	1978	
7616	UWV616S	Bristol VRT/SL3/6LXB	Eastern Coach Works	CO43/31F	1978	Ex Southdown, 1991
7621	UWV621S	Bristol VRT/SL3/6LXB	Eastern Coach Works	CO43/31F	1978	
7623	UWV623S	Bristol VRT/SL3/6LXB	Eastern Coach Works	CO43/31F	1978	

7650-7685   Bristol VRT/SL3/6LB   Eastern Coach Works   H43/31F   1980-81 7655 rebodied 1983

7650	XJJ650V	7658	XJJ658V	7665	XJJ665V	7672	BJG672V	7679	CJJ679W
7651	XJJ651V	7659	XJJ659V	7666	XJJ666V	7673	BJG673V	7680	SKL680X
7652	XJJ652V	7660	XJJ660V	7667	XJJ667V	7674	BJG674V	7681	SKL681X
7653	XJJ653V	7661	XJJ661V	7668	XJJ668V	7675	BJG675V	7682	SKL682X
7654	XJJ654V	7662	XJJ662V	7669	XJJ669V	7676	CJJ676W	7683	SKL683X
7655	XJJ655V	7663	XJJ663V	7670	XJJ670V	7677	CJJ677W	7684	SKL684X
7657	XJJ657V	7664	XJJ664V	7671	BJG671V	7678	CJJ678W	7685	SKL685X

7746-7755   MCW Metrobus 2 DR132/11   MCW   H46/31F   1988

7746	E746SKR	7748	E748SKR	7750	E750SKR	7752	E752SKR	7754	E754UKR
7747	E747SKR	7749	E749SKR	7751	E751SKR	7753	E753SKR	7755	E755UKR

7761-7767   MCW Metrobus 2 DR132/15   MCW   DPH43/27F   1989

7761	F761EKM	7763	F763EKM	7765	F765EKM	7767	F767EKM
7762	F762EKM	7764	F764EKM	7766	F766EKM		

7771-7775   MCW Metrobus 2 DR132/14   MCW   H46/31F   1989

7771	F771EKM	7772	F772EKM	7773	F773EKM	7774	F774EKM	7775	F775EKM

7781	F781KKP	Scania N113DRB	Alexander RH	H47/33F	1989
7782	F782KKP	Scania N113DRB	Alexander RH	H47/33F	1989

7801-7810   Leyland Olympian ON2R56C16Z4   Northern Counties   H51/34F   1990

7801	H801BKK	7803	H803BKK	7805	H805BKK	7807	H807BKK	7809	H809BKK
7802	H802BKK	7804	H804BKK	7806	H806BKK	7808	H808BKK	7810	H810BKK

7811	J811NKK	Leyland Olympian ON2R50C13Z4	Northern Counties Countybus Palatine	H47/30F	1992
7812	J812NKK	Leyland Olympian ON2R50C13Z4	Northern Counties Countybus Palatine	H47/30F	1992
7813	J813NKK	Leyland Olympian ON2R50C13Z4	Northern Counties Countybus Palatine	H47/30F	1992
7814	J814NKK	Leyland Olympian ON2R50C13Z4	Northern Counties Countybus Palatine	H47/30F	1992

7821-7830   Leyland Olympian ON2R50C13Z4   Northern Counties Countybus Palatine   H47/30F   1993

7821	K821TKP	7823	K823TKP	7825	K825TKP	7827	L827BKK	7829	L829BKK
7822	K822TKP	7824	K824TKP	7826	L826BKK	7828	L828BKK	7830	L830BKK

7973-7990 Bristol VRT/SL3/6LXB   Willowbrook   H43/31F 1978

| 7973 | RVB973S | **7978** | RVB978S | **7988** | TFN988T |
| 7974 | RVB974S | **7982** | TFN982T | **7990** | TFN990T |

8192	XSU912	MCW Metroliner HR131/2	MCW Hilner	C49FT	1984	Ex Premier Travel, Cambridge, 1988
8211	D211VEV	Scania K112CRB	Berkhof Esprite 350	C41FTL	1987	
8243	SIB8243	Volvo B10M-60	Plaxton Paramount 3500 3	C49FT	1991	Ex Park, Hamilton, 1993
8245	LDZ3145	MCW Metroliner HR131/6	MCW Hiliner	C49FT	1985	Ex Premier Travel, Cambridge, 1988
8246	XYK976	MCW Metroliner HR131/6	MCW Hiliner	C49FT	1985	Ex Premier Travel, Cambridge, 1988
8399	XDU599	MCW Metroliner HR131/1	MCW Hiliner	C49FT	1983	Ex MCW, Birmingham, 1988
8837	BKR837Y	Leyland Leopard PSU3G/4R	Eastern Coach Works B51	DP47F	1982	
8838	TSU638	Leyland Tiger TRCTL11/3R	Plaxton Paramount 3200Exp	DP51F	1983	
8839	TSU639	Leyland Tiger TRCTL11/3R	Plaxton Paramount 3200Exp	DP53F	1983	
8840	TSU640	Leyland Tiger TRCTL11/3R	Plaxton Paramount 3200Exp	DP53F	1983	
8841	TSU641	Leyland Tiger TRCTL11/3R	Plaxton Paramount 3200Exp	DP53F	1983	
8842	TSU642	Leyland Tiger TRCTL11/3R	Plaxton Paramount 3200Exp	DP53F	1983	
8850	WSU450	MCW Metroliner CR126/8	MCW	C51F	1984	
8851	WSU451	MCW Metroliner CR126/8	MCW	C51F	1984	
8852	WSU452	MCW Metroliner CR126/8	MCW	C51F	1984	
8854	E854UKR	MCW Metroliner HR131/12	MCW Hiliner	C51F	1988	
8855	E855UKR	MCW Metroliner HR131/12	MCW Hiliner	C51F	1988	
8856	J856NKK	Scania K93CRB	Plaxton Paramount 3500 3	C49FT	1992	

8901-8908 Volvo B10M-60   Plaxton Expressliner   C49FT   1989

| 8901 | G901PKK | **8903** | G903PKK | **8905** | G905PKK | **8907** | G907PKK |
| 8902 | G902PKK | **8904** | G904PKK | **8906** | G906PKK | **8908** | G908PKK |

8909	J909NKP	Volvo B10M-60	Plaxton Expressliner	C49FT	1992	
8910	K910TKP	Volvo B10M-60	Plaxton Première 350	C49FT	1993	
8996	PFN873	Bova FHD12-280	Bova Futura	C49FT	1986	Ex Marinair, Canterbury, 1991

SPECIAL EVENTS VEHICLES

0135	CD7045	Leyland G7	Short (1926)	O27/24RO	1922	Ex preservation, 1970
0409	409DCD	Leyland Titan PD3/4	Northern Counties	FCO39/30F	1964	
0424	424DCD	Leyland Titan PD3/4	Northern Counties	FCO39/30F	1964	
0770	HKE690L	Bristol VRT/SL2/6LX	Eastern Coach Works	O43/34F	1973	Ex Maidstone & District, 1983
0813	UF4813	Leyland Titan TD1	Brush	O27/24RO	1929	
0946	MFN946F	AEC Regent V 3D3RA	Park Royal	H40/32F	1967	Ex East Kent, 1983

Previous registrations

BYJ919Y	XUF534Y, 404DCD
HUF451X	RUF434X, XLD244
JNJ194V	HFG924V, DSV943
LDZ3145	B245JVA
MSU466	D526ESG
NFX667	HHC367Y
OUF262W	JWV125W, LYJ145
PFN873	C996FKM
SYC852	JWV126W
TSU638	FKK838Y
TSU639	FKK839Y
TSU640	FKK840Y
TSU641	FKK841Y
TSU642	FKK842Y
USV672	FKL172Y
UWP105	XUF535Y
VSV564	FKL171Y
WSU450	B850TKL
WSU451	B851TKL
WSU452	B852TKL
XDU599	A543WOB, ABM399A
XSU912	B192JVA
XYK976	B246JVA
YLJ332	RUF432X

400DCD	RUF430X
401DCD	XUF531Y
402DCD	XUF532Y, 2880CD
403DCD	XUF533Y
405DCD	RUF435X
406DCD	RUF436X
407DCD	RUF437X
408DCD	LPN358W
410DCD	RUF438X
411DCD	RUF431X
412DCD	TGF222X
413DCD	HHC364Y
415DCD	RUF429X
416DCD	F816CWJ
417DCD	F817DWG
418DCD	E518YWF
419DCD	F565HPP
420DCD	RUF433X, MSV533
424DCD	424DCD, AOR158B
495FFJ	B193CGA
896HOD	B192CGA

Named vehicles
7805 Odyssey, 7807 Enterprise, 7810 Thomas Becket

Special liveries
East Sussex County Rider : 2891/2
Freedom Coach for the Disabled : 8211
National Express : 1008/66, 8901-10/96
Overall advertisements : 3, 10/1/3, 20, 43, 51/5, 68, 74, 83, 86, 129/32/9, 246, 347, 1184, 1893, 1900, 7661/74/82/4, 7748, 7809, 7988, 8837
Derwyn's Tours : 1001
Canterbury Park and Ride : 1401-3, 7801

SUSSEX BUS

Sussex Bus Ltd, 11 June Close, Bognor Regis, West Sussex, PO21 4UH

Sussex Bus was founded by John Belson of Partridge Green, Sussex, in the summer of 1985, to operate a number of bus services into Brighton from the rural areas to the north-west. Contracts were soon gained from West Sussex County Council, taking vehicles to Haywards Heath, Horsham and Worthing at weekends. From the outset the fleet was characterised by vehicles carrying advertising for the local Evening Argus newspaper, whose colours inspired the distinctive red and white livery.

In January 1989 a substantial block of West Sussex contract services were obtained in the Chichester area, following withdrawal by Yellowline Coaches, and the bulk of the company's work now focuses in this area. From June 1993 the company launched City Legs, a ten-minute circular service around Chichester, and half-hourly route 270 from Chichester to Parklands Estate, using Iveco minibuses in an eye-catching livery. The City Legs service has since developed through support from Tesco following the opening of their superstore at Fishbourne in September 1993.

SUSSEX BUS

XSU682	Leyland Leopard PSU3B/4R	Willowbrook Warrior(1990)	B49F	1973	Ex Danks, Oldfield, 1991
SSU780W	Leyland Leopard PSU3E/4R	Duple Dominant	B55F	1973	Ex Graham, Paisley, 1990
CSY978	Leyland Leopard PSU3B/4R	Willowbrook Warrior(1988)	B55F	1975	Ex Crowther, Morley, 1992
JTM109V	AEC Reliance 6U2R	Duple Dominant	B53F	1979	Ex Tillingbourne, 1992
CSU992	Leyland Leopard PSU3E/4R	Willowbrook Warrior(1990)	B47F	1979	Ex SUT, 1990
XSU612	Leyland Leopard PSU3F/4R	Willowbrook Warrior(1990)	B48F	1981	Ex Battrick, Blackburn, 1990
D130LTA	Renault S56	Reeve Burgess	B23F	1986	Ex Plymouth, 1993
D143LTA	Renault S56	Reeve Burgess	B23F	1986	Ex Plymouth, 1993
D552HNW	Iveco Daily 49.10	Robin Hood City Nippy	B21F	1986	Ex Pickford, Grittleton, 1992
D475WPM	Iveco Daily 49.10	Robin Hood City Nippy	B21F	1986	Ex Stagecoach South, 1993
D624BCK	Iveco Daily 49.10	Robin Hood City Nippy	B25F	1986	Ex Ribble, 1993
E306FYJ	Iveco Daily 49.10	Robin Hood City Nippy	B25F	1988	Ex Wright, Worthing, 1994
E307FYJ	Iveco Daily 49.10	Robin Hood City Nippy	B25F	1988	Ex Wright, Worthing, 1994
F651RBP	Iveco Daily 49.10	Robin Hood City Nippy	B25F	1989	Ex Midhurst Hospital, 1993

Previous registrations

CSU992	OMA506V, TCS157	XSU612	PWT238W
CSY978	HWY718N, CSU934	XSU682	OKG158M

TAPPIN'S COACHES

Tom Tappin Ltd, Holiday House, Station Road, Didcot, Oxfordshire, OX11 7LZ

Tappin's is a long established coach operator with a regularly updated fleet of vehicles for holiday tours all over Britain and more local work. A bus service was introduced in 1991 to the Thames Valley Business Park, on which the Dennis Dart is a regular performer. A number of contract services are also operated. A modern depot at Southmead Industrial Estate, Didcot, houses most of the fleet. Other vehicles are kept at the Station Road address.

Four of the six full-size single-deckers of the Sussex Bus fleet are Leyland Leopards rebodied by Willowbrook. These have brought some stability to what was an often-changing fleet. The registration of CSU992 effectively disguises its 1979 origins in this view. Malcolm King

One of only two single-deck buses in the large Tappins fleet, J854PUD is a Dennis Dart purchased in 1992 with Reeve Burgess bodywork shortly before production was transferred to the main Plaxton site. Malcolm King

TAPPINS COACHES

OMW979	Bedford YMT	Plaxton Supreme III	C53F	1978	
399OME	Bedford YMT	Plaxton Supreme III	C53F	1979	
SGF965	Bedford YMT	Plaxton Supreme III	C53F	1979	
WOA521	Bedford YMT	Plaxton Supreme III	C53F	1979	
CGL849	Bedford YMT	Plaxton Supreme III	C53F	1979	
875EPX	Volvo B58-56	Plaxton Supreme IV	C53F	1980	
415OPF	Volvo B58-56	Plaxton Supreme IV	C53F	1980	
704BYL	Volvo B58-56	Plaxton Supreme IV	C53F	1980	
21DGX	Volvo B58-56	Plaxton Supreme IV	C53F	1980	
34BCG	Volvo B58-56	Plaxton Supreme IV	C53F	1980	
7368MK	Volvo B58-61	Plaxton Supreme IV	C51F	1981	
YJB121	Volvo B10M-61	Plaxton Supreme V	C53F	1982	
966MKE	Volvo B10M-61	Plaxton Supreme V	C53F	1982	
461XPB	Volvo B10M-61	Plaxton Viewmaster IV	C53F	1982	
500EFC	Volvo B10M-61	Plaxton Viewmaster IV	C53F	1982	
653GBU	Leyland National 2 NL116AL11/1R		B52F	1982	Ex AERE, Harwell, 1991
579CIM	Volvo B10M-61	Plaxton Paramount 3500	C49FT	1984	
XKX94	Volvo B10M-61	Plaxton Paramount 3500	C49FT	1984	
3818NU	Volvo B10M-61	Plaxton Paramount 3500	C53F	1984	
XGW911	Volvo B10M-61	Plaxton Paramount 3500	C53F	1984	
B161FWJ	Volvo B10M-61	Plaxton Paramount 3500 2	C53F	1985	
B162FWJ	Volvo B10M-61	Plaxton Paramount 3500 2	C53F	1985	
B163FWJ	Volvo B10M-61	Plaxton Paramount 3500 2	C53F	1985	
B164FWJ	Volvo B10M-61	Plaxton Paramount 3500 2	C53F	1985	
C323UFP	Volvo B10M-61	Plaxton Paramount 3500 2	C53F	1986	
C324UFP	Volvo B10M-61	Plaxton Paramount 3500 2	C53F	1986	
C325UFP	Volvo B10M-61	Plaxton Paramount 3500 2	C53F	1986	
KBZ7145	Ford Transit	Carlyle	B16F	1986	Acquired 1994
C326UFP	Volvo B10M-61	Plaxton Paramount 3500 2	C49FT	1986	
D73HRU	Volvo B10M-61	Plaxton Paramount 3500 3	C53F	1987	
D74HRU	Volvo B10M-61	Plaxton Paramount 3500 3	C53F	1987	
D75HRU	Volvo B10M-61	Plaxton Paramount 3500 3	C53F	1987	
E257PEL	Toyota HB31R	Caetano Optimo	C19F	1988	
E258PEL	Toyota HB31R	Caetano Optimo	C19F	1988	
E260PEL	Volvo B10M-61	Plaxton Paramount 3500 3	C53F	1988	
E471SON	MCW Metrobus 2 DR102/63	MCW	H45/30F	1988	Ex London Buses, 1992
IIL1832	Auwaerter Neoplan N122/3	Auwaerter Skyliner	CH57/18DT	1988	Ex Stockdale, Selby, 1992
F165XLJ	Volvo B10M-60	Plaxton Paramount 3500 3	C53F	1989	
F166XLJ	Volvo B10M-60	Plaxton Paramount 3500 3	C53F	1989	
F400DUG	Volvo B10M-60	Plaxton Paramount 3500 3	C48FT	1989	Ex Wallace Arnold, 1993
G417YAY	Volvo B10M-60	Plaxton Paramount 3500 3	C53F	1990	
G418YAY	Volvo B10M-60	Plaxton Paramount 3500 3	C53F	1990	
G419YAY	Volvo B10M-60	Plaxton Paramount 3500 3	C53F	1990	
G504LWU	Volvo B10M-60	Plaxton Paramount 3500 3	C50F	1990	Ex Wallace Arnold, 1993
G505LWU	Volvo B10M-60	Plaxton Paramount 3500 3	C50F	1990	Ex Wallace Arnold, 1993
G507LWU	Volvo B10M-60	Plaxton Paramount 3500 3	C50F	1990	Ex Wallace Arnold, 1993
G506LWU	Volvo B10M-60	Plaxton Paramount 3500 3	C50F	1990	Ex Wallace Arnold, 1993
G508LWU	Volvo B10M-60	Plaxton Paramount 3500 3	C50F	1990	Ex Wallace Arnold, 1993
G509LWU	Volvo B10M-60	Plaxton Paramount 3500 3	C50F	1990	Ex Wallace Arnold, 1993
G510LWU	Volvo B10M-60	Plaxton Paramount 3500 3	C50F	1990	Ex Wallace Arnold, 1993
G511LWU	Volvo B10M-60	Plaxton Paramount 3500 3	C50F	1990	Ex Wallace Arnold, 1993
G512LWU	Volvo B10M-60	Plaxton Paramount 3500 3	C50F	1990	Ex Wallace Arnold, 1993
G513LWU	Volvo B10M-60	Plaxton Paramount 3500 3	C50F	1990	Ex Wallace Arnold, 1993
H261GRY	Volvo B10M-60	Plaxton Paramount 3500 3	C53F	1991	
H262GRY	Volvo B10M-60	Plaxton Paramount 3500 3	C53F	1991	
J854PUD	Dennis Dart 9.8SDL3012	Reeve Burgess Pointer	B43F	1992	
K301GDT	Volvo B10M-60	Van Hool Alizée	C53F	1993	
K302GDT	Volvo B10M-60	Van Hool Alizée	C53F	1993	

Previous registrations

CGL849	YAN823T	WOA521	YAN822T	704BYL	DJB865V	653GBU	WBW735X
IIL1832	E480YWJ	XGW911	A420CJH	579CIM	A417CJH	399OME	YAN814T
KBZ7145	D826UTF	XKX94	A418CJH	21DGX	DJB863V		
OMW979	TJH252S	YJB121	NBL903X	500EFC	NBL905X		
SGF965	YAN821T	34BCG	DJB866V	875EPX	DJB864V		

THAMES TRANSIT GROUP

Thames Transit Ltd, Belgrave Road, Exeter, Devon, EX1 2AJ

Thames Transit, part of the Transit Holdings group based at Exeter, started operations in Oxford on 7th March 1987 with a half-hourly coach service between Oxford and London marketed as 'Oxford Tube'. This has subsequently been increased in frequency and extended in London to Victoria. A minibus service in Oxford started from the same date and the network has been further expanded since, notably through the acquisition of South Midland from City of Oxford Motor Services in December 1988. The operating area now extends to Aylesbury, Eynsham and Witney. The Oxford fleet is based at Cowley (Horspath Road), Chipping Norton and Witney.

Blue Admiral started trading on 25th May 1991, covering local services in the Portsmouth area. This followed the introduction of Thames Transit operations in that area on 20th January 1991 as a result of the Monopolies & Mergers Commission directive to Stagecoach Holdings to divest itself of its Portsmouth operations. The fleet is based at Hilsea West.

Red Admiral also started trading on 25th May 1991, covering out-of-town services in the Portsmouth area as well as local work at Gosport and Hilsea. The fleet is based at Havant and Fareham.

The local services of all three fleets were for a long while based on standard Ford Transit/Mellor machines, although updating has taken place with Mercedes-Benz vehicles. More recently Ivecos and Dennis Darts with dual-door bodywork have been introduced. The Red Admiral fleet also includes two open-top Leylands, and the Oxford fleet includes coaches for the London services.

Inter-fleet exchanges occur regularly with other members of the group. A new livery is being introduced of silver grey with dark blue and red relief. Oxford Tube coaches operate in a distinctive livery of red with grey relief.

One of two survivors of the Portsmouth fleet inherited by the group, No.287 is a Leyland Atlantean with Alexander bodywork of the style long associated with the area. This view at Clarence Pier, Southsea shows it operating for Blue Admiral on a local service linking historical sites. David Harman

The Thames Transit group took several Mercedes-Benz minibuses with Mellor bodywork in the early 1990s. No.358 turns a corner in Worcester Street, Oxford on 19th February 1994.
Keith Grimes

Replacement of the original Ford Transit/Mellor minibuses forged ahead from 1992 with the purchase of Mercedes-Benz with dual-door Mellor bodies. No.2049 prepares to leave Portsmouth Hard on Blue Admiral work.
A. J. Simpkins

Amongst the latest group arrivals are fourteen Dennis Darts with dual-door Plaxton bodywork for the Blackbird Leys service at Oxford. No.3005 demonstrates the special livery used for this service.
David Harman

Left **From the 1991 batch of Mercedes-Benz with Carlyle bodywork, No.400 is in the Red Admiral fleet.**
Calvin Churchill

The Oxford Tube service has proved constantly successful, and the fleet has been regularly updated on an annual basis. The 1994 arrivals are two Volvos with Jonckheere coachwork.
Colin Lloyd

THAMES TRANSIT GROUP (Blue Admiral, Red Admiral, Thames Transit fleets)

1	L723JUD	Volvo B10M-60		Jonckheere Deauville P599	C49FT	1994		
2	L724JUD	Volvo B10M-60		Jonckheere Deauville P599	C49FT	1994		

3-7		Volvo B10M-60	Jonckheere	C49FT	1993

3	L210GJO	4	L211GJO	5	L212GJO	6	L213GJO	7	L214GJO

9	D142PTT	Leyland Tiger TRCTL11/3RH	Plaxton Paramount 3500 2	C51FT	1987	
10	PYV277	Leyland Tiger TRCTL11/3RZ	Plaxton Paramount 3500 2	C51FT	1986	Ex Devon General, 1987
11	LSV670	Leyland Tiger TRCTL11/3RZ	Plaxton Paramount 3500 2	C51FT	1986	Ex Devon General, 1987
15	C922HYA	Leyland Tiger TRCTL11/3RZ	Plaxton Paramount 3200 2	C49FT	1986	Ex Southern National, 1989
16	B896YYD	Leyland Tiger TRCTL11/3RH	Plaxton Paramount 3500	C48FT	1985	Ex Devon General, 1990
17	B894YYD	Leyland Tiger TRCTL11/3RH	Plaxton Paramount 3500	C48FT	1985	Ex Devon General, 1990
18	L159LBW	Volvo B10M-62	Jonckheere Deauville	C49FT	1994	
19	H913FTT	Volvo B10M-60	Ikarus Blue Danube	C49FT	1991	
20	H914FTT	Volvo B10M-60	Ikarus Blue Danube	C49FT	1991	
21	L155LBW	Volvo B10M-62	Jonckheere Deauville	C49FT	1994	
22	H916FTT	Volvo B10M-60	Ikarus Blue Danube	C49FT	1991	
23	H917FTT	Volvo B10M-60	Ikarus Blue Danube	C49FT	1991	
24	J499MOD	Volvo B10M-60	Ikarus Blue Danube	C49FT	1992	
25	H914PTG	Volvo B10M-60	Ikarus Blue Danube	C49FT	1991	Ex Hills, Tredegar, 1992
26	H915PTG	Volvo B10M-60	Ikarus Blue Danube	C49FT	1991	Ex Hills, Tredegar, 1992

27	H916PTG	Volvo B10M-60	Ikarus Blue Danube	C49FT	1991	Ex Hills, Tredegar, 1992
28	H917PTG	Volvo B10M-60	Ikarus Blue Danube	C49FT	1991	Ex Hills, Tredegar, 1992
29	L156LBW	Volvo B10M-62	Jonckheere Deauville	C49FT	1994	
30	L157LBW	Volvo B10M-62	Jonckheere Deauville	C49FT	1994	
31	L158LBW	Volvo B10M-62	Jonckheere Deauville	C49FT	1994	

49-91

Mercedes-Benz 709D   Reeve Burgess   DP25F   1988   Ex Devon General, 1989*
* 65/7 ex Bayline, 1994

| 49 | F749FDV | 52 | F752FDV | 61 | F721FDV | 67 | F727FDV | 91 | F761FDV |
| 50 | E829ATT | 53 | F713FDV | 65 | F725FDV | 79 | F739FDV | | |

97	AFJ741T	Bristol LH6L	Plaxton Supreme III Exp	C41F	1979	Ex Devon General, 1997
98	A103JUD	Ford Transit	Dormobile	B16F	1983	Ex South Midland, 1987
99	B105XJO	Ford Transit	Carlyle	B16F	1985	Ex South Midland, 1987

100-141

Ford Transit VE6   Mellor   B16F   1986-87

100	D100PTT	106	D106PTT	122	D122PTT	129	D129PTT	136	D136PTT
101	D101PTT	107	D107PTT	123	D123PTT	130	D130PTT	137	D137PTT
102	D102PTT	108	D108PTT	124	D124PTT	132	D132PTT	138	D138PTT
103	D103PTT	109	D109PTT	126	D126PTT	133	D133PTT	139	D139PTT
104	D104PTT	115	D115PTT	127	D127PTT	134	D134PTT	140	D140PTT
105	D105PTT	121	D121PTT	128	D128PTT	135	D135PTT	141	D776NDV

201-222

Ford Transit VE6   Mellor   B16F   1987-88 223 ex Bayline, 1994

201	E201BDV	206	E206BDV	213	E213BDV	218	E218BDV	222	E222BDV
202	E202BDV	207	E207BDV	214	E214BDV	219	E219BDV		
203	E203BDV	208	E208BDV	215	E215BDV	220	E220BDV		
204	E204BDV	212	E212BDV	217	E217BDV	221	E221BDV		

252-259

Ford Transit VE6   Mellor   B16F   1988

| 252 | F752BDV | 255 | F755FDV | 257 | E197BDV | 259 | E199BDV |
| 253 | F753FDV | 256 | E196BDV | 258 | E198BDV | | |

| 287 | XTP287L | Leyland Atlantean AN68/1R | Alexander AL | H45/30D | 1973 | |

300-324

Mercedes-Benz 709D   Reeve Burgess Beaver   DP25F   1988   Ex South Midland, 1988

300	E300BWL	305	E305BWL	310	F310EJO	315	F315EJO	320	F320EJO
301	E301BWL	306	E306BWL	311	F311EJO	316	F316EJO	321	F321EJO
302	E302BWL	307	E307BWL	312	F312EJO	317	F317EJO	322	F322EJO
303	E303BWL	308	E308BWL	313	F313EJO	318	F318EJO	323	F323EJO
304	E304BWL	309	E309BWL	314	F314EJO	319	F319EJO	324	F324EJO

325-346

Mercedes-Benz 709D   Reeve Burgess Beaver   B25F   1989

325	F775FDV	328	F765FDV	331	F768FDV	344	F402KOD
326	F776FDV	329	F766FDV	332	F769FDV	345	F403KOD
327	F764FDV	330	F767FDV	333	F770FDV	346	F746FDV

347-354

Mercedes-Benz 709D   Carlyle   B29F   1990

| 347 | G947TDV | 349 | G949TDV | 351 | G951TDV | 353 | G953TDV |
| 348 | G948TDV | 350 | G950TDV | 352 | G952TDV | 354 | G954TDV |

355-366

Mercedes-Benz 811D   Carlyle   B29F   1990   Ex Bayline, 1992/3

355	G831UDV	358	G834UDV	361	G837UDV	364	G840UDV
356	G832UDV	359	G835UDV	362	G838UDV	365	G841UDV
357	G833UDV	360	G836UDV	363	G839UDV	366	G842UDV

367-400

Mercedes-Benz 811D   Carlyle   B29F   1991

367	H985FTT	373	H991FTT	379	H997FTT	385	H176GTA	396	H787GTA
368	H986FTT	374	H992FTT	380	H171GTA	386	H177GTA	397	H788GTA
369	H987FTT	375	H993FTT	381	H172GTA	387	H178GTA	400	H101HDV
370	H988FTT	376	H994FTT	382	H173GTA	388	H179GTA		
371	H989FTT	377	H995FTT	383	H174GTA	391	H782GTA		
372	H990FTT	378	H996FTT	384	H175GTA	392	H783GTA		

636-656

636-656	Ford Transit 190D		Mellor		B16F	1987	646 ex Bayline, 1994		

636	D636NOD	**641**	D641NOD	**645**	D645NOD	**651**	D651NOD	**655**	D655NOD
638	D638NOD	**643**	D643NOD	**646**	D646NOD	**653**	D653NOD	**656**	D656NOD

773-823	Ford Transit VE6		Mellor		B16F	1987-88			

773	F773FDV	**793**	D793NDV	**807**	E807WDV	**817**	E817WDV
782	D782NDV	**794**	D794NDV	**808**	E808WDV	**819**	E819WDV
783	D783NDV	**795**	D795NDV	**809**	E809WDV	**820**	E820WDV
788	D788NDV	**798**	D798NDV	**811**	E811WDV	**821**	E821WDV
789	D789HDV	**803**	E803WDV	**814**	E814WDV	**822**	E822WDV
791	D791NDV	**805**	E805WDV	**815**	E815WDV	**823**	E823WDV
792	D792NDV	**806**	E806WDV	**816**	E816WDV		

824	E824WDV	Ford Transit VE6	Mellor	B16F	1988	Ex Devon General, 1991
955	F24PSL	Iveco Daily 49.10	Robin Hood	B23F	1989	Ex Magicbus, Perth, 1990
956	D618BCK	Iveco Daily 49.10	Robin Hood	B21F	1987	Ex Ribble, Preston, 1991
957	D939ECR	Iveco Daily 49.10	Robin Hood	B19F	1986	Ex Hampshire Bus, 1990
958	D937ECR	Iveco Daily 49.10	Robin Hood	B19F	1986	Ex Magicbus, Perth, 1990

959-973	Iveco Daily 49.10		Robin Hood		B23F	1988			

959	E959LPX	**962**	E962LPX	**965**	E965LPX	**968**	E968LPX	**971**	E971LPX
960	E960LPX	**963**	E963LPX	**966**	E966LPX	**969**	E969LPX	**972**	E972LPX
961	E961LPX	**964**	E964LPX	**967**	E967LPX	**970**	E970LPX	**973**	E973LPX

993	F603CET	Leyland Tiger TRBTL11/2RP	Plaxton Derwent	B54F	1988	Ex Kelvin Central, 1993
994	F604CET	Leyland Tiger TRBTL11/2RP	Plaxton Derwent	B54F	1988	Ex Kelvin Central, 1993

995-999	Leyland Tiger TRBTL11/2RP		Plaxton Derwent		B54F	1988	Ex Burton, Brixham, 1989-90		

995	F278HOD	**996**	F279HOD	**997**	F280HOD	**998**	F281HOD	**999**	F282HOD

2000-2084	Iveco Daily 49.12		Mellor Duet		B26D	1993-94	2029-32/70-2 ex Bayline, 1993		

2000	K701UTT	**2015**	K716UTT	**2030**	K731UTT	**2045**	K922VDV	**2060**	L312BOD
2001	K702UTT	**2016**	K717UTT	**2031**	K732UTT	**2046**	K923VDV	**2061**	L313BOD
2002	K703UTT	**2017**	K718UTT	**2032**	K724UTT	**2047**	K928VDV	**2062**	L314BOD
2003	K704UTT	**2018**	K719UTT	**2033**	L322BOD	**2048**	K929VDV	**2063**	L315BOD
2004	K705UTT	**2019**	K720UTT	**2034**	L323BOD	**2049**	K930VDV	**2064**	L316BOD
2005	K706UTT	**2020**	K721UTT	**2035**	L324BOD	**2050**	K931VDV	**2065**	L317BOD
2006	K707UTT	**2021**	K722UTT	**2036**	K911VDV	**2051**	K801WFJ	**2067**	L319BOD
2007	K708UTT	**2022**	K723UTT	**2037**	K912VDV	**2052**	K802WFJ	**2068**	L320BOD
2008	K709UTT	**2023**	K913VDV	**2038**	K914VDV	**2053**	K918VDV	**2070**	K924VDV
2009	K710UTT	**2024**	K725UTT	**2039**	K915VDV	**2054**	K619XOD	**2071**	K926VDV
2010	K711UTT	**2025**	K726UTT	**2040**	K916VDV	**2055**	K621XOD	**2072**	K927VDV
2011	K712UTT	**2026**	K727UTT	**2041**	K917VDV	**2056**	K622XOD	**2081**	K806WFJ
2012	K713UTT	**2027**	K728UTT	**2042**	K919VDV	**2057**	K919WFJ	**2082**	K633XOD
2013	K714UTT	**2028**	K729UTT	**2043**	K920VDV	**2058**	K623XOD	**2083**	K816WFJ
2014	K715UTT	**2029**	K730UTT	**2044**	K921VDV	**2059**	L311BOD	**2084**	K620XOD

3000-3013	Dennis Dart 9.8SDL		Plaxton Pointer		B39D	1994			

3000	L709JUD	**3003**	L712JUD	**3006**	L715JUD	**3009**	L718JUD	**3012**	L721JUD
3001	L710JUD	**3004**	L713JUD	**3007**	L716JUD	**3010**	L719JUD	**3013**	L722JUD
3002	L711JUD	**3005**	L714JUD	**3008**	L717JUD	**3011**	L720JUD		

Vintage bus

(2)	LRV992	Leyland Titan PD2/12	Metro-Cammell	O33/26R	1956	Ex Southdown, 1991

Previous registrations

LSV670	C129KJO	PYV277	C128KJO

Named vehicles

9 Magdalen, 11 Queens, 15 St Catherine's

THANET BUS

G.C. Chisholm, 18 Northdown Road, Cliftonville, Margate, Kent, CT9 2RW

Thanet Bus has developed from local bus operations introduced by Chisholm in the Isle of Thanet during 1988. These initially led to keen competition with East Kent, although both parties withdrew to a compatible position in March 1990. Subsequently Thanet Bus gained Kent County Council contracts covering former East Kent work from Ramsgate to the westerly villages, and for a short period weekday evening and Sunday work for the main service linking Canterbury with Thanet towns. From June 1994 a more recent service from Canterbury via Sandwich, Ramsgate, Broadstairs and Margate to Westgate has been reformed as a complete loop to and from Canterbury via Upstreet, sharpening again the competitive edge with what is now Stagecoach East Kent.

The original midibuses were largely supplanted by a variety of second-hand single-deckers, chiefly Leyland Nationals, in the early 1990s. More recently these have been replaced by Mercedes-Benz midibuses, operating in a white and red livery. The fleet is garaged at Wingham.

Thanet Bus have introduced Mercedes-Benz midibuses over the past two years to replace their Leyland Nationals. Like most of the vehicles, G380FSF came from Scotland. This view catches it at Cecil Square, Margate nearing the end of its journey to Westgate. Alan Simpkins

THANET BUS

C488DKN	Renault S56	Dormobile	B26F	1985	Ex Lytham, St Columb, 1987
D125NUS	Mercedes-Benz L608D	Alexander AM	B21F	1986	Ex Kelvin Central, 1992
D127NUS	Mercedes-Benz L608D	Alexander AM	B21F	1986	Ex Duncan, Kinloch Rannoch, 1994
D134NUS	Mercedes-Benz L608D	Alexander AM	B21F	1986	Ex Kelvin Central, 1992
D139NUS	Mercedes-Benz L608D	Alexander AM	B21F	1986	Ex Kelvin Central, 1992
E899YKO	Renault S56	Dormobile	DP24F	1988	
G380FSF	Mercedes-Benz 811D	PMT	DP33F	1990	Ex Caldwell, Greenock, 1992
H541NSF	Mercedes-Benz 811D	PMT	DP33F	1990	Ex Caldwell, Greenock, 1992
H899NFS	Mercedes-Benz 811D	PMT	DP33F	1990	Ex Caldwell, Greenock, 1992
L206MAV	Mercedes-Benz 709D	Marshall	B27F	1993	

TILLINGBOURNE

Tillingbourne Bus Co Ltd, Littlemead Estate, Alford Road, Cranleigh, Surrey, GU6 8ND

Tillingbourne Bus Company dates back to 1924 when Mr G. Trice, a country carrier based in Chilworth near Guildford, started motor bus operation under the name of Tillingbourne Valley Services. A Guildford town service started in 1931 and lasted for 40 years. A limited company was formed in 1935 and since 1972 has run under its own title.

Activities extended into Sussex in 1972 when North Downs Rural Transport ceased, Tillingbourne taking the Horsham and Rusper circular service. A separate company, Tillingbourne (Sussex) Ltd was formed in May 1974 to administer this operation. Tillingbourne expanded again in 1981 when services in the Orpington and East Croydon areas were taken over from Orpington & District. These were handed over to Metrobus in September 1983. The Surrey Hills and Sussex Weald services were revised in November 1982 following the takeover of Tony McCann Coaches of Forest Green.

The present network consists of a variety of services in the Guildford, Cranleigh, Fleet, Farnborough, Horsham, Reigate and Crawley areas. A new livery of dark yellow with dark blue relief is being introduced, replacing the former blue, white and yellow. The main garage is at Cranleigh with subsidiary sites at Horsham and Aldershot.

Amongst a variety of minibuses in the Tillingbourne fleet is J431PPF, an Iveco Daily with Carlyle bodywork new in 1991 shortly before that firm went out of business. This view was taken in Aldershot in April 1994. Ivor Norman

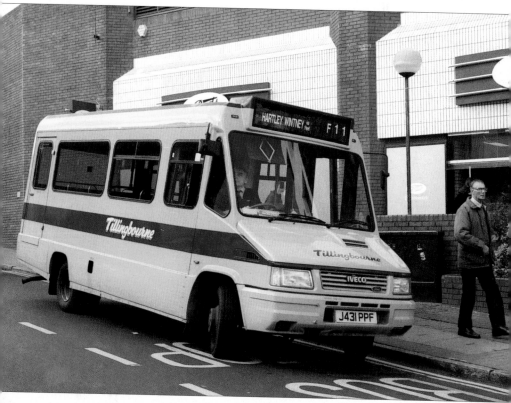

H421GPM is a Mercedes-Benz 709D with Dormobile Routemaker bodywork. The photographer caught it at Aldershot in April 1994, setting out on the rural trip to Reading. Ivor Norman

Tillingbourne's 1993 order-book called for two Volvos with Plaxton bodywork, represented by K102XPA at Guildford Bus Station. Two further Volvos arrived in 1994, this time with Northern Counties bodywork. Malcolm King

TILLINGBOURNE

Reg	Chassis	Body	Seating	Year	Notes
ODV404W	AEC Reliance 6U2R	Duple Dominant II Express	C53F	1981	Ex Metrobus, 1991
508AHU	Volvo B10M-56	Plaxton Supreme V Express	C53F	1982	Ex James & Williams, Treorchy, 1989
JTF971W	Leyland National 2 NL116AL11/1R		B52F	1981	Ex Farmer, Ashford, 1992
LFX502	Volvo B58-61	Plaxton	C53F	1981	Ex British Aerospace, Kingston, 1993
FGD827X	Volvo B10M-56	Duple Dominant	B51F	1982	Ex Graham, Paisley, 1990
NIW5983	Volvo B10M-61	Plaxton	C53F	1982	Ex Goodwin, Stockport, 1994
OHE271X	Volvo B10M-61	Plaxton	C53F	1982	Ex Goodwin, Stockport, 1994
FOD942Y	Dennis Dorchester SDA802	Wadham Stringer Vanguard	B59F	1983	
FOD943Y	Dennis Dorchester SDA802	Wadham Stringer Vanguard	B59F	1983	
A889FPM	Bedford YMT	Plaxton Bustler	B55F	1984	
A339HNR	Volvo B10M-56	Plaxton Paramount 3200Exp	C53F	1984	Ex Woodstone, Kidderminster, 1988
B877OLJ	Leyland Tiger TRCTL11/2R	Duple Dominant	B55F	1984	
TBC658	Volvo B10M-61	Plaxton Paramount 3500	C53F	1984	Ex Ford, Gunnislake, 1990
B327KPD	Bedford YMT	Plaxton Bustler	B53F	1984	
B918NPC	Bedford YMQ	Lex Maxeta	B37F	1985	Ex The Bee Line, 1988
B919NPC	Bedford YMQ	Lex Maxeta	B37F	1985	Ex Alder Valley South, 1987
C195WJT	Leyland Tiger TRBL11/2R	Duple Dominant	B53F	1985	
D424XPJ	Iveco Daily 49.10	Robin Hood	B21F	1986	
D425XPJ	Iveco Daily 49.10	Robin Hood	B21F	1986	
D694WAU	Bedford YMT	Plaxton Derwent II	B55F	1987	Ex Felix, Stanley, 1988
D603RGJ	Bedford YMT	Plaxton Derwent II	B53F	1987	Ex Cheney, Banbury, 1994
D293XUF	Volvo B10M-46	Plaxton	B33F	1987	Ex Terminus, Crawley, 1994
E216MFX	Bedford YMT	Plaxton Derwent II	B53F	1987	
E523TOV	Iveco Daily 49.10	Carlyle	B21F	1987	Ex Marchwood, Totton, 1992
E364NEG	Volvo B10M-61	NC Paladin (1992)	B51F	1988	Ex County, 1991
E215MFX	Bedford YMT	Plaxton Derwent II	B53F	1988	
F870TLJ	Leyland Tiger TRBTL11/2RP	Plaxton Derwent II	B52F	1988	
F222AKG	Iveco Daily 49.10	Carlyle	B21F	1988	Ex Cynon Valley, 1993
F224AKG	Iveco Daily 49.10	Carlyle	B21F	1988	Ex Cynon Valley, 1993
F193TNP	Volvo B10M-61	Ikarus	C49FT	1988	Ex Shorthouse, Droitwich, 1994
F914TBP	Mercedes-Benz 709D	Robin Hood City Nippy	C25F	1989	Ex Tenby Bus & Coach, 1991
G401DPD	Scania K93CRB	Plaxton Derwent II	B57F	1989	
G402DPD	Iveco Daily 49.10	Carlyle Dailybus 2	B25F	1989	
G403DPD	Iveco Daily 49.10	Carlyle Dailybus 2	B25F	1989	
G404DPD	Iveco Daily 49.10	Carlyle Dailybus 2	B25F	1989	
G405DPD	Iveco Daily 49.10	Carlyle Dailybus 2	B25F	1989	
G406DPD	Iveco Daily 49.10	Carlyle Dailybus 2	B25F	1989	
G256NCK	Mercedes-Benz 814D	Reeve Burgess Beaver	C33F	1990	Ex Kerridge, Brighton, 1992
G810DPH	Iveco Daily 49.10	Phoenix	B25F	1990	
H421GPM	Mercedes-Benz 709D	Dormobile Routemaker	B27F	1990	
H422GPM	Mercedes-Benz 709D	Phoenix	B27F	1990	
H423GPM	Mercedes-Benz 709D	Phoenix	B27F	1990	
H426KPA	Mercedes-Benz 811D	Dormobile Routemaker	B29F	1991	
H427KPA	Mercedes-Benz 811D	Dormobile Routemaker	B29F	1991	
H428KPA	Mercedes-Benz 811D	Whittaker-Europa	B28F	1991	
H429KPA	Mercedes-Benz 811D	Whittaker-Europa	B28F	1991	
H11TBC	Volvo B10M-60	Ikarus Blue Danube	C53F	1991	
J430PPF	Mercedes-Benz 709D	Dormobile Routemaker	B29F	1991	
J431PPF	Iveco Daily 49.10	Carlyle Dailybus 2	B25F	1991	
K101XPA	Volvo B10M-55	Plaxton Derwent II	B55F	1993	
K102XPA	Volvo B10M-55	Plaxton Derwent II	B55F	1993	
L103EPA	Volvo B6-50	NC Countybus Paladin	B40F	1994	
L104EPA	Volvo B6-50	NC Countybus Paladin	B40F	1994	

Previous registrations

LFX502	FTH992W	TBC658	A298XUK, 353TPF, A489YGL
NIW5983	LWN125X	508AHU	NUH262X

Named vehicles

B918NPC Lord Hayman of Reigate, D424 XPJ Will, D425XPJ Rose, G401DPD The Lord Billy, G404DPD Frodo, G810DPH Fredegar

Special liveries

Overall advertisement B327KPD
Dorking Coaches TBC658, NIW5983

TOWN & AROUND

Town & Around (Folkestone) Ltd, 5 Thanet Gardens, Folkestone, Kent, CT19 6DE

In October 1986 Robert Miller started a local service in Folkestone between Holywell Avenue and Broadmead Village. The network was expanded in March 1988 with the acquisition of Kent County Council contracts for weekday routes 558 and 559 between Hythe and Canterbury through Stelling Minnis and a Sunday route from Folkestone to Maidstone, although these were lost in the 1990 round of re-tendering. Instead, Kent County Council route 593 from Dover (Western Heights) to Martin was gained from April 1990. Other local services have since been introduced in Folkestone and Hythe, though on a complementary rather than competitive basis with East Kent.

The present company was authorised in November 1989, reflecting the trading name which had been used since inception. The fleet is in a smart livery of white with blue skirt and light blue stripes.

TURNER'S

T.C. Turner (Turner's of Maidstone), 9 Charlton Lane, West Farleigh, Maidstone, Kent, ME15 0NX

Turner's commenced bus operations in July 1990, working on the route from Maidstone to Coxheath, on which a significant presence is still maintained. Other work includes school contracts in the Maidstone area.

The fleet is based at the Wouldham site of Farleigh Coaches, and is operated in various as-acquired liveries.

WEALDEN-BEELINE

Wealden PSV Ltd, Badsell Road, Five Oak Green, Tonbridge, Kent, TN12 6QY

Wealden PSV has developed an increasing presence in local bus operation in recent years, and now operates several routes in the Tonbridge and Tunbridge Wells area, some of these on a co-ordinated basis with East Surrey and Fuggles. A Kent Karrier network is also operated under local authority contract in Tonbridge. The fleet of Beeline, Southborough was acquired early in 1989 and led to the introduction of a service from Tunbridge Wells to Heathfield, part of which is operated under contract to East Sussex County Council; on summer Sundays this is extended to provide a service from Wateringbury to Eastbourne.

The fleet has included a number of unusual vehicles loaned or transferred from the associated dealing firm, Wealden PSV Sales. The basic fleet livery is two shades of green with cream relief.